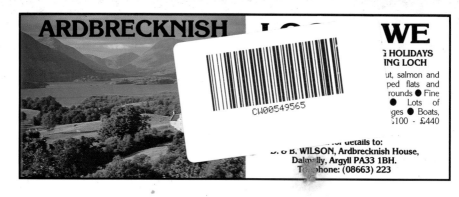

Please mention this Pastime Publications Guide

CATCH HIM ON VIDEO.

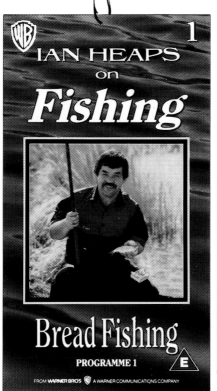

Ian Heaps on Fishing

A SERIES OF 6 VIDEOS DESIGNED TO IMPROVE YOUR FISHING TECHNIQUES

1. Bread Fishing. 2. The Waggler. 3. The Slider. 4. The Feeder. 5. Long Pole: Lake. 6. Long Pole: River.

AVAILABLE NOW　　WARNER HOME VIDEO
Trademark of Warner Bros. Inc. A TIME WARNER COMPANY　　**ONLY £9.99 EACH**

At Sea Life Centres people of all ages can discover the amazing marine life that lives from the surface of our seas down to the ocean depths.

Now, you too can experience life in a way usually seen only by an underwater diver, meeting hundreds of sea creatures, all native to Britain, face to face — without actually getting cold and wet!

Our aim is to create an awareness of the marine environment at a time when it is under greater threat from man than ever before.

Sea Life Centres — Pioneering...

Imagine the bottom of the ocean. There was a time when only deep sea divers knew how it felt to walk there but now everyone can experience this unforgettable sensation. Surrounded by water, creatures glide past before your eyes. Sea Life Centres technical advances have extended the boundaries of displaying marine life. New types of glass and acrylic provide unique, uninterrupted views and give a real insight into life beneath the waves.

Sea Life Centres — Inspiring...

A pool where you can actually touch. Here you have a chance to discover the colour and beauty of rockpool life — with someone never too far away to answer the hundreds of questions that everyone has. Turning exploration into discovery, interest into enthusiasm and questions into answers. Understanding and respect will ensure a safer future for the seas.

Sea Life Centres — Caring...

SEALWATCH — Experienced staff at our Scottish centres have developed Rear and Release programmes over the past decade. Each year they provide round the clock feeding and care for abandoned seal pups, who will return safely back to the wild after several months. Releasing pups helps supplement seal populations which are at the mercy of pollution and disease.

**Sea Life Centres — Pioneering... Inspiring... Caring...
For The Future!**

CONTENTS

Gazetteer — Rivers, Lochs & Sea Angling

Cover Design by Artisan Graphics, Edinburgh. Cover photograph by Chris Hall Photography. Fishing equipment kindly lent by John Dickson & Son Ltd, Edinburgh.

Pastime Publications Ltd gratefully acknowledge the assistance of The Scottish Tourist Board, Area Tourist Boards, and others in compiling this guide.

First published by The Scottish Tourist Board 1970
Typesetting by Outline
Printed & Bound in the U.K.

**Worldwide distribution by
The British Tourist Authority**

BTA

INDEX

ALSO SEE COLOUR ADVERTS

USEFUL ADDRESSES IN SCOTTISH SPORT FISHERIES

Scottish Tourist Board, 23 Ravelston Terrace, Edinburgh EH4 3EU.
Tel: 031-332 2433.

Department of Agriculture & Fisheries for Scotland, Pentland House, 47 Robb's Loan, Edinburgh EH14 1SQ.
Tel: 031-556 8400.

Inspector of Salmon Fisheries, Pentland House (Room 227), 47 Robb's Loan, Edinburgh EH14 1TW.
Tel: 031-244 6227.

Freshwater Fisheries Laboratory, Officer in Charge, Pitlochry PH16 5LB.
Tel: (0796) 2060.

Marine Laboratory, P.O. Box 101, Victoria Road, Aberdeen AB9 8DB.
Tel: (0224) 876544.

Secretary, Scottish River Purification Boards Association, City Chambers, Glasgow G2 1DU.
Tel: 041-227 4190.

Scottish Sports Council, Caledonia House, South Gyle, Edinburgh EH12 9DQ.
Tel: 031-317 7200.

Nature Conservancy Council, 12 Hope Terrace, Edinburgh. EH9 2AS.
Tel: 031-447 4784.

Forestry Commission, Jill Mackay, Information Officer, 231 Corstorphine Road, Edinburgh EH12 7AT.
Tel: 031-334 0303.

North of Scotland Hydro-Electric Board, 16 Rothesay Terrace, Edinburgh EH3 7SE.
Tel: 031-225 1361.

Institute of Fisheries Management, Secretary (Scottish Branch), Gordon Struthers, "Torshavn", Lettoch Road, Pitlochry PH16 5AZ.
Tel: (Home) 0796 2846 (Work) 0796 2060.

Anglers' Cooperative Association, Secretary, Iain Mackenzie, 46 Ormidale Terrace, Edinburgh EH12 6EF.
Tel: 031-337 7587.

The Salmon and Trout Association, Sec. G. Bentinck, Burgh House, 7/9 King St, Aberdeen AB2 3AA.
Tel: (0224) 645046.

Scottish Anglers' National Association, Secretary, Mr. A.D. Jamieson, 5 Cramond Glebe Road, Edinburgh EH4 6ND.
Tel: 031-229 9292, ext. 2559.

Central Scotland Anglers' Association, Secretary, Kevin Burns, 53 Fernieside Crescent, Edinburgh.
Tel: 031-664 4685.

Federation of Highland Angling Clubs, Secretary, W. Brown, Coruisk, Strathpeffer, Ross-shire.
Tel: (0997) 21446.

Department of Forestry and Natural Resources, University of Edinburgh, Kings Buildings, Mayfield Road, Edinburgh EH9 3JU.
Tel: 031-667 1081.

Institute of Aquaculture, University of Stirling, Stirling FK9 4LA.
Tel: (0786) 73171.

The effects of **POLLUTION** may take years to disappear from a river

REPORT ALL CASES IMMEDIATELY

Keep samples of dead fish

Please telephone

Forth River Purification Board

031-441 1674 (24 hours) or 0786 51741

or **Forth District Salmon Fishery Board** *0836 722 647*

or your local **Police Office**

A BASKET OF GAME FISHING

by Bruce Sandison

SCOTLAND has some of the finest game fishing in the world; most of it is easily accessible, readily available and relatively inexpensive. The secret of success is preplanning. Knowing where and when to go.

The 1991 edition of 'Scotland for Game, Sea and Coarse Fishing' will help you along the way to finding your ideal holiday location; further details regarding salmon, trout and sea-trout fishing in Scotland may be found in 'The Trout Lochs of Scotland', 3rd Edition, published by Unwin Hyman @ £9.95, and 'Game Fishing in Scotland', published by Mainstream @ £14.95.

The following notes give details of a few 'special' places; where, over the past forty years, my family and I have had wonderful holidays; where we have always managed to catch a few, and even more have got away.

Not just holidays fishing for salmon, trout and sea-trout, but also where we have enjoyed the wild beauty of the mountains and moorlands of my native land; secret glens and hidden mountain lochans; magnificent lochs, surrounded by fertile, well-cultivated fields; fine fisheries, full of hard-fighting, superb, wild brown trout.

However, if you are the sort of angler who measures success in terms of numbers caught, or size of fish, read no further: the holidays I describe are not for you. You will be happier on a well-managed, put-and-take, lowland fishery, chasing a 'limit bag'.

My type of fishing regards the capture of fish as no more than a bonus: be it a spring-silver salmon, fresh from Atlantic feeding grounds, or a brace of perfectly matched brown trout from a distant hill loch.

Of equal importance to me is the setting, scenery and wildlife: curlew, calling hauntingly over the moor; a shy dipper, black and white, best-bib-and-tuckered, darting in the clear waters of some mountain stream; curious, Flow Country otters, in east Sutherland; red deer haughtily marking your progress across the hill.

This is what game fishing means to me. If you agree, then you may find that some of my suggested locations are of interest. If they do not meet your expectations, then I apologise in advance: one man's angling paradise is another man's fishing nightmare.

Nevertheless, I believe there is a single irrefutable, rationale for fishing: 'Deus nobis haec otia fecit'. A god gave us this leisure. Make the most of that gift, and Tight Lines and happy days in all your efforts.

CAITHNESS is mainland Scotland's most northerly county; a gentle landscape, scattered with a series of some of the finest trout lochs in Scotland: Watten, containing wild brown trout of the highest quality. A boat on Watten, with two rods fishing, will cost in the region of £8.00.

St. John's, a well managed fishery, stocked with native fish, reared in the Angling Association's own hatchery to preserve the genetic integrity of the species. Cost for a day and evening, boat and two rods is £14.00.

Dour Loch Heilen costs £10.00 per day for a boat and two rods; fish of under 2 lb should be returned to the water, to fight another day; Calder costs £8.00 per day, for a boat with two rods fishing, and is full of free-rising 'traditional' Highland trout averaging 8oz - and the odd monster, waiting to catch you unawares.

These are the principal fisheries, all easily accessible, but there are many more, both remote and accessible, available to visitors; little Loch Stemster, the ideal place for a family picnic, where you may park the car close to the lochside and find great sport whilst children splash in the shallows, or explore the surrounding countryside.

Loch Ruard, an invigorating stumble, west from Stemster, where trout average 12oz and fight like fish twice their size; where you may meet otters, and almost certainly, red throated divers.

Rangag, by the roadside, the perfect place to take newcomers to the 'gentle art' of fly-fishing - they are bound to catch fish. Allow approximately £10.00 per day, for boat and two rods fishing on these smaller waters.

With the exception of Loch Calder, where spinning and bait fishing is allowed, every loch in Caithness is strictly fly-fishing only. You must obtain proper permission, before fishing.

Obey these simple rules and you will be made welcome. Most anglers do. A curse on the few, greedy, inconsiderate 'fish-mongers' who don't: they are a disgrace to themselves and to our sport.

Caithness trout fishing can be very good in May, but always be prepared to wrestle with high winds: a drouge and an outboard motor are essential on these exposed waters.

June is perhaps the 'prime' month, and again in September. Nevertheless, if you are committed to having your annual fishing holiday in July or August, fear not - Caithness wild brown trout still provide great sport.

You will find details of names, addresses and telephone numbers of where to book boats in the main directory of this guide. Further details of accommodation may be obtained from the Caithness Tourist Board, Whitechapel Road, Wick, Caithness. Telephone: (0955) 2596.

Caithness also has one of the best salmon streams in the north, the Thurso River, which produces some 1000 fish each season. The river is divided into thirteen principal beats, each fishing two rods; and during the course of the week, anglers fish a different beat each day, allowing visitors to enjoy the whole river.

Thurso fishing is generally let by the week. Expert advice and assistance is available from the Fishery Manager, Eddie MaCarthy, and gillies are available to guide you to where the fish lie.

Not so productive, but just as delightful, is the Wick River, where most seasons produce upwards of 300 salmon; a total that would put many better-known beats to shame. But the Wick River is entirely dependent upon good water levels to give of its best. At times, in high-summer, it almost disappears, and it's possible to cross dry-shod, in carpet slippers.

However, after heavy rain, sport can be fast and furious: nor does it cost an arm and a leg. 1990 charges were: adult visitor, per day, £8.00; per week, £25.00. Under 16 years of age, OAP's and disabled visitors, £2.00 per day, £8.00 per week. Perhaps the best-for-money salmon fishing in Scotland.

Permission to fish the Wick River may be obtained from Hugo Ross, Tackle Shop, 16 Breadalbane Terrace, Wick. Tel: (0955) 4200. Hugo Ross is an experienced angler and will be able to advise on tackle, techniques and tactics.

He also has a marvellous selection of suitable flies, both for salmon and trout fishing; and two boats, with outboard engines, for visitors fishing Loch Watten.

The other principal Caithness salmon stream is the Forss River, which flows northwards from Loch Shurrery, reaching the sea in Crosskirk Bay, six miles to the

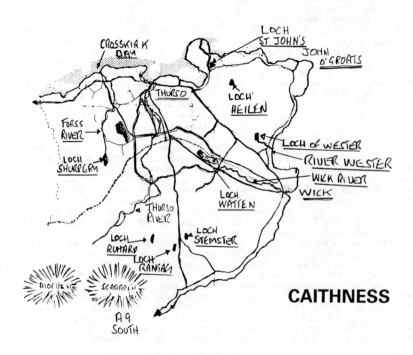

CAITHNESS

west of Thurso. The best fishing on Forss is to be found in the lower three miles, from Lythmore Strath to the sea; and most seasons produce 100/150 salmon.

The peak month is September, but given good water levels, the early part of the year can also produce good results. During the second week of July, 1990, 27 Atlantic-fresh, silver salmon were landed.

The river has been time-shared and is restricted to eight rods fishing two four-rod beats, changing over at lunch time. When owners are not using their rod, it is often possible to rent a week on Forss and the cost varies, from £250/£400 per rod per week depending upon the time of year.

The best time for Caithness salmon fishing depends upon personal preference. Spring runs, for which the Thurso River in particular was noted, have been much reduced in recent years. August and September offer the greatest numbers of fish. However, early season salmon fishing is far less expensive, and, in my opinion, one April fish is worth about ten Autumn salmon, both from the point of view of quality and, more important, the strength with which they fight.

Caithness is a wonderful location for a fishing holiday, family or otherwise; empty beaches at Dunnet and Reiss for the bucket-and-spade brigade, backed by magnificent sand dunes which provide good shelter from the prevailing wind.

Stunning, ruined, cliff-top castles; three good links golf courses, at Reiss, Thurso and Reay; pony trekking, bird watching and hill-walking; a magnificent array of 4,500 year old, Neolithic monuments. Something for every member of the family - and game fishing of outstanding quality.

NORTH UIST appears to be more water than land. There are hundreds of freshwater lochs, most containing wild brown trout, and also several excellent sea-trout and salmon systems.

Nor can there be many more lovely places to fish: desolate, heather-clad moorlands, scattered with a shining array of lochs and lochans where you may wander among the hills all day without meeting another soul.

Northwards, in the distance, are the peaks of Harris: Roineabhal (460m), Bhoiseabhal (374m), Greabhal (280m) and Mula (271m). Southwards lie the graceful mountains of South Uist: Hecla (606m), Ben Corodale (527m) and shapely Beinn Mhor (608m).

Game fishing in North Uist is managed by the Department of Agriculture and Fisheries for Scotland, and the North Uist Estate, who let much of their fishing to the Lochmaddy Hotel; a comfortable angling hotel that has been caring for fishermen for more than 100 years.

Of the many brown trout lochs, three DAFS lochs in particular deserve special mention: Loch an Armuinn, Deadman's Loch, and Loch an Duin; because they hold much larger fish than many of their neighbours. You will have to work a lot harder to catch them, but could be rewarded with trout of up to 3lbs for your trouble.

There is a Dun on a narrow promontory in the south west corner of this interlinked chain of lochs; North Uist has more than its fair share of these Iron Age forts for there are more than 100, scattered throughout North Uist, in easily defensible positions; on small islands or long peninsulas.

A boat is available and this provides the easiest method of getting round the many corners and crooked bays that enclose the loch. However, to reach Loch Armuinn you will have to abandon ship at the north end of Loch an Duin and take to the heather, since only a small stream joins it to the main body of the loch.

The North Uist Estate also has really first class wild brown trout fishing. The shoreline of Loch Scadavay meanders in and out, round headlands and corners, for a distance of some fifty miles. There are reputed to be 365 islands in the loch, one for each day of the year; and many of these even have their own small lochan.

Loch Obisary is one of my favourite North Uist waters, overlooked by Eaval, the island's highest mountain. From either boat or bank, Obisary will give endless pleasure and the quality of fish is simply superb. However, if you are bank fishing, take great care for the water deepens quickly from the shore. Stay back, and safe, below the skyline: fish lie close to the bank.

One of the most exciting waters is Loch nan Geireann, situated in the north of the island, close to the convenient A865 which circles North Uist. There are several islands in the loch and on one, Eilean-an-Tighe, Neolithic pottery remains have been excavated. The dig yielded so much that it's probable that the kilns on the island supplied most of the Hebrides with pottery.

On Loch nan Geireann the angler has the best of all worlds: excellent quality wild brown trout, hard-fighting sea-trout, and sea-lice covered salmon. This is also where the great raptors soar, and there is a good chance that you will see golden eagle.

Indeed, the bird life of North Uist is as exciting as the game fishing. Listen for the rusty-engined coughing of corncrake; the red-necked phalarope nests in the Balranald Nature Reserve; golden plover, redshank, greenshank, oyster catcher, grey-lag geese, black throated and red throated divers; always something to please the eye and gladden the heart.

Such as the North Uist sea-trout lochs. The 1989 season produced almost 300 fish and most of these were taken from Loch Horisary, to the west of the island. Fish arrive from July onwards, with August providing best sport.

On the south shore of Horisary, fish the area east and west of the old fence that enters the loch, close to the bank. On the north shore, there is an iron post: from there, westwards to the mouth of the outlet burn should produce fish, again, close to the shore. Few sea-trout are taken in the middle of the loch.

Sea-trout can also be caught in the sea. The Geirann sea-pool is perhaps the most productive, and certainly, in my opinion, the most beautiful. Fishing is possible for an hour or so on either side of low tide. Walk out, over the sands, to where white-fringed, green waves end their long Atlantic journey. At times the pool is packed with returning fish: both sea-trout and salmon.

West from Geirann, between Valley Island and Griminish, are more sea-trout pools. These fish are heading for Loch nan Clachan, adjacent to the road. Turning south, at Ardhisker, there are other sea-trout waters, waiting to tempt you: Vausasry, Trosavat, Dusary: and the sea-pools between Claddach Kyles and Kirkbost Island.

However, be warned, there are quicksands along the way, and the tide could catch you unawares. Always seek local advice, regarding route and timing. Even better, if possible, go with a local angler, or hire the services of one of the excellent gillies who work from the Lochmaddy Hotel.

The most productive salmon system on North Uist is the Skealtar System, a few minutes' drive from the Lochmaddy Hotel and Ian McIlwraith, the owner, will point you to where the fish lie.

There are six principal lochs in the system: Loch na Ciste, Loch nan Geireann (not to be confused with the larger water of the same name already mentioned), Lower Skealtar, Upper Skealtar, North Scadavay and Loch nan Eun.

Best sport is had on Geireann and Lower and Upper Skealtar, and in recent years salmon of over 15lbs have been caught. Ian McIlwraith works hard to improve his fishing and each year fish are introduced from the Estate hatchery to the headwaters of the system.

More than 80 salmon are now taken each season, averaging 8lb in weight, and they fight furiously, at times stripping the reel down to the backing in their first, wild rush. Excellent boats are maintained on Skealtar but to have the best opportunity of hooking a fish it is advisable to ask for the services of a gillie, at least for the first few days of your visit.

On Loch nan Geirann, the place to concentrate is where the little stream tumbles in from Skealtar. A footbridge crosses the flow and salmon lie close in, by the weeds, as the stream sweeps into the loch. Stay well back: fish the stream from one position, lengthening your line, rather than walking forward.

On Lower Skealtar, the best drift is from the mouth of the inlet burn from Upper Skealtar, in an 'S' shape, aiming to arrive on the north side of the little island. Upper Skealtar fish may also be found in the most south easterly bay, and to the south of the small islands.

NORTH UIST

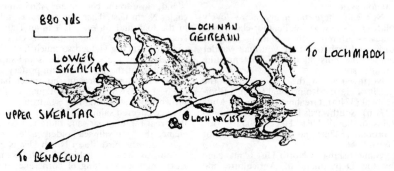

Standard pattern Scottish loch flies work well for salmon, sea-trout and brown trout. Take along a selection including: Invicta, Silver Invicta, Blue Zulu, Black Zulu, Black Pennel, Ke-He, Soldier Palmer, March Brown and Butchers.

Permission to fish the DAFS trout lochs on North Uist may be obtained from: The Area Office, Balivanich, Benbecula. Tel: (0870) 2346, and costs a few pounds per rod per day for bank fishing, and approximately £10.00 per day for a boat with two rods fishing.

For details of self-catering accommodation on North Uist, write to: Western Isles Tourist Board, 4 South Beach Street, Stornoway, Isle of Lewis, Outer Hebrides. Tel: (0851) 3088.

For travel details, contact: Loganair Ltd., Glasgow Airport, Abbotsinch, Paisley. Tel: 041-889 3181; or Caledonian MacBrayne, The Ferry Terminal, Gourock. Tel: (0457) 34531. Whatever way you decide to travel, get there as soon as you can. Fine sport in fine surroundings awaits your arrival.

COIGACH. From Muir of Ord, north of Inverness, follow the road to Ullapool; past the Falls of Rogie and Loch Garve along the A835, by grey, windswept Loch Glascarnoch.

Ullapool was built by the British Fishery Society in 1788 to exploit the ever growing demand for herring - the principal food for slaves in the plantations of the West Indies.

But due to the wild, rocky nature of the coastline and unpredictability of the arrival of herring, Ullapool never gained the same stature as a herring fishing station as Wick, or the east coast centres along the Moray Firth.

Nevertheless, even today Ullapool boasts a sizeable fishing fleet and plays host to many foreign vessels hunting the rich waters of the western Atlantic for prey and pay.

Ullapool is the gateway to the Coigach or Ross, a fifth part of Ross & Cromarty. In Roman times, Ptolemy noted that it was inhabited by the Carini tribe. In the days of Norse domination, the north of Scotland was known as the Province of Cat: hence Caithness, the eastern part and Suderland, Sutherland, the south land of Vikings.

Hardy people still stalk the hills and moorlands of Coigach and Inverpolly but with different ambitions, for the area is a wilderness of delight for climber, hill walker, naturalist - and game fisherman.

Accommodation is easy to find and ranges from good hotels to welcoming B & B establishments. But I prefer the freedom of self-catering, and there are several first-class cottages, particularly at Achiltibuie, overlooking the glorious Summer Isles.

Good game fishing abounds. Exciting, accessible, roadside trout lochs such as Lurgainn, Bad a'Ghaill, Raa and Vatachan; and first class sea-trout fishing on Loch Oscaig and the little River Garvie.

For the angler who likes a long walk with his fishing, there are numerous, rarely fished hill lochs, nestling among the high crags and corries; all holding bright, hard-fighting little fish, and a few waters which contain trout of 3lbs and more.

The two largest lochs are Lurgainn and Bad a'Ghaill, bounded on the north by the little road from Drumrunie on the A835 to Achiltibuie, so access is very easy.

Lurgainn is four miles long by up to half a mile wide and drops to a depth of 156ft near the eastern end; Bad a'Ghaill is two miles in length and nearly three quarters of a mile wide.

The lochs are linked by Loch Bad na h'Achlaise, the Green Loch. At times of high water levels a boat may be hauled over the sand bar from either Lurgainn or Bad a'Ghaill in order to fish h'Achlaise.

In spite of their proximity to the road neither loch is heavily fished; it is the exception, rather than the rule to see any boats out; and to see more than one boat would be extraordinary.

Therefore, it is difficult to be accurate regarding what you are likely to catch. One thing is certain, both waters contain large stock of typical Highland trout which weigh in the order of 8/12oz and on a good day large baskets of fish are common.

But there are much larger fish, lurking in the depths; and they generally remain there because no-one really bothers to spend time looking for them. These large trout, ferox, are caught by trolling, and from time to time local anglers catch superb specimens.

If you feel inclined to try your luck/skill, pay particular attention to the east end. Two feeder burns enter the loch here and you should fish this area very carefully.

Concentrate also round the small islands, taking care to avoid the sunken rocks, just below the surface to the east of the first islet.

Lurgainn narrows towards the west end and a long shelf of rock extends out under the water from the north shore. This is reputed to be the best trolling area and over the years some very large fish have been taken here.

Further westwards, in the last main south-shore bay, another feeder burn enters and this area can also offer great sport.

Bad a'Ghaill has a reputation of being dour but it is fished so infrequently that I think this reputation is ill-deserved. The most productive areas are where the stream enters from the Green Loch, and at the west end, where Bad A'Ghaill exits down a

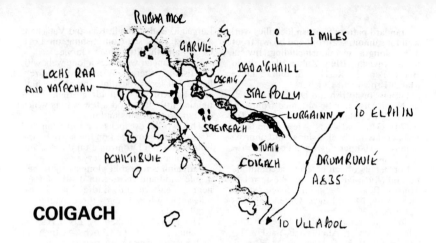

COIGACH

delightful little river to Loch Oscaig.

Loch Oscaig is the most western of the waters lying adjacent to the Drumrunie/Achiltibuie Road. The loch is one and a quarter miles long by up to three quarters of a mile wide. The rocky River Garvie drains the loch near the north east end, tumbling under the road and reaching the sea within a few hundred yards.

Before entering Garvie Bay, the river extends into a sizeable, weedy loch; this can provide wonderful sport with sea-trout from July onwards. A stone's throw from the tiny loch is one of the most beautiful beaches in Scotland; a wide sweep of shining sands facing northwards towards the mountains of Assynt.

Sea-trout make the short journey from the sea to Loch Oscaig with ease and the north end of Oscaig produces the best sport. Another good area to try is in the tree-lined south bay and along the south west shore.

Remember, sea-trout are fidgety creatures that tend to roam; so it is often a case of going to them, rather than waiting for them to come to you. If you do find them, be prepared for some wonderful action: sea-trout of up to 7lbs are taken most seasons.

To the south of Lurgainn, Bad a'Ghaill and Oscaig lies a wild desolate mountain land where you may walk all day without meeting another soul.

This is the home of red deer, wildcat, otter and fox; the lochs host red and black throated divers, golden eye, mergansers and terns; wild flowers scatter the moorlands and from the summit an amazing panorama awaits.

South and westwards, across the sparkling Summer Isles the horizon is lined by dramatic peaks: Cuillins on Skye, Harris and Lewis hills, the gentle 'Heather Isles';

An Teallach, above destitution Road in the Fisherfield Forest.

Northwards, across the Inverpolly National Nature Reserve, lies Suilven, Ben More Assynt, Quinag; the long, grey shoulder of Canisp, graceful Stac Polly, Cul Mor and Cul Beg.

The most dramatic of the Coigach hill lochs is Lochan Tuath, a blue sheet below the massive bulk of Sgurr an Fhidleir; but a less taxing, and just as rewarding day out can be made to the group of lochs to the north east of the Summer Isles Hotel.

After an invigorating tramp of about an hour you will reach Lochan Sgeireach, where you should have little difficulty in catching breakfast for the following day. To the east of Sgeireach lie three other small waters, all well worth a visit: Leacach, Fada and Ballach.

On Rubha Mor, the western section of the Coigach Peninsula, there are even more lochs for you to explore. Clar Loch Mor, Clar Loch Beag and Loch na Totaig are the principal lochs and getting to them will stretch both legs and lungs.

But it is well worth the effort, for this is the stuff that fishing dreams are made of. Leave the car at Achanhaird and forget the world for a day. Coigach and Inverpolly offer all that makes fishing important to me: solitude, scenery, bird-song and silence; and the ever-present, happy sound of rising trout.

Details of where to obtain permission are given in the appropriate section of the guide. Information about self-catering accommodation can be obtained from the Wester Ross Tourist Information Office, Ullapool. Tel: (0854) 2135. You should make your booking well in advance. Most properties are already fully booked by the end of April.

ARDTORNISH & MORVERN

"Eirich agus tiugainn, O." Get up and come along! Such was the Gaelic invitation to visit Morvern, issued by Dr. Norman Macleod, the minister of St. Columba Church in 1810; and the invitation is still as welcoming today.

Morvern is a gentle, anglers' paradise of snow-covered mountains, sparkling lochans, wild moorlands and tumbling streams; ancient woodlands, spring-busy with nesting birds; primrose nodding in sunny corners, dipper darting in crystal-clear torrents; the haunting call of curlew on the hill.

Morvern is one of Scotland's least visited areas because even today it is relatively inaccessible. The quickest way in is by the short ferry crossing over Loch Linnie at Corran Narrows, eight miles south from Fort William.

From there, for most of the way, you are in the grip of a tortuous, single-track road; climbing through Glen Tarbert, down to the head of Loch Sunart, winding up from the sea between Beinn nam Beathrach and Taobh Dubh, into Gleann Geal.

Ardtornish lies at the head of sea-loch Aline and the original estate, known as Achranich, was purchased in 1845 by Octavious Smith, a London distiller. Eventually, through acquisition and marriage, Achranich was combined with Ardtornish Estate and the whole property became known as Ardtornish.

The River Aline, meaning "the short river" is one of the most delightful salmon streams in Scotland: deep pools, turbulent runs and easy to fish. It is a classic Highland spate river and depends very much upon water levels to give of its best.

Most seasons see upwards of 45 salmon and some 180 sea-trout landed, the majority being caught during August and September. Mac's Pool recently produced a fine salmon weighing 20lbs 3oz and Mr. P. Dale took 12 fish during one week, including a lovely 18lbs hen salmon which was carefully returned; allowing her to go about her proper business: propagating the species.

The river banks are well maintained and fishing is restricted to a maximum of twelve rods per day on six beats, rotating throughout the week to allow everyone the best possible chance of sport.

Wading is not necessary. Indeed, it is best to keep well back from the bank when fishing, to avoid 'spooking' the salmon. Use a 10/11ft rod and a floating line, saying the proper prayers and crossing the right fingers!

The most successful flies for salmon include: Black Pennel, Blue Charm, Silver Invicta, Yellow Torrish, Green Highlander, Prawn Fly, and Hairy Mary. Vary the size according to prevailing water levels.

There are four designated Sites of Special Scientific Interest on the estate, including the John Raven Memorial Nature Reserve, and more than 136 different species of birds have been recorded. Golden eagle are present and it is often possible to see them, particularly by Loch Arienas.

Arienas is a delightful loch to fish and offers a good alternative if water levels in the River Aline make salmon fishing problematical. Brown trout thrive and both boat and bank fishing bring results.

The west shore line is best and most accessible for bank fishing, offering relatively comfortable wading. The water has that golden, peat-stained, Highland colour and fish cruise into the clear shallows to grab the well-presented fly.

The wooded east shore is best tackled from a boat and you should concentrate your attack around the mouths of the seven feeder burns that tumble down from the steep slopes of Beinn na h-Uamaha. On a warm June night when the air is loud with the buzz of insects, that is the place to be: fingers crossed, net ready.

Sandy Hutchinson was, during 1989, and was rewarded with two fine trout for his efforts: 5lbs 8 oz, and 4lbs. The heaviest fish to be taken from the loch was a magnificent sea-trout weighing 10lbs, also taken during 1989.

North of Arienas is another good brown trout water, Loch Doire nam Mart, peaty and weed fringed. The fish here tend to average about 8oz but towards the end of the season there is always the chance of a sea-trout forcing its way up from Arienas through the little feeder burn that joins the two lochs.

Ardtornish is a welcoming place with the emphasis on providing everything for a relaxing holiday for every member of the family. Bicycles with baby seats on the back are available for hire. There are good laundry facilities and even a lending library for fireside evenings.

John Hodgson rents out canoes, sailing dinghies, rowing boats and outboard powered boats. And if you fancy catching your own supper in Loch Aline, John will even provide the necessary tackle, prawn creels and bait.

Comfortable accommodation is available both in the magnificent Ardtornish House, or in a number of beautifully situated estate cottages, amongst the woodlands, by the river bank and along the sea-shore.

Most of the old Morvern woodlands were destroyed in 1745 during the Jacobite rebellion, when General Campbell ordered the "wasting" of Morvern. The work was carried out by Captain Robert Duff RN with marines and sailors from the sloops Terror and Princess Anne. Forests were set

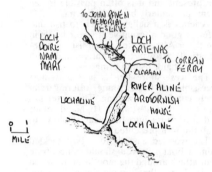

ARDTORNISH

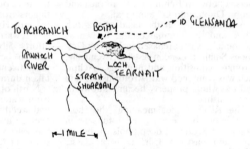

alight from Drimmin in the west to Ardtornish, a distance of eleven miles.

However, gracious woodlands survive today, the famous Ardtornish Gardens: twenty eight acres of superb parkland, lawns, shrubs and trees, by the shores of Loch Aline. The woodlands are magnificent: native birch, firs and pines, dark green against the pink sandstone of Ardtornish House.

But the rhododendrons are the most spectacular aspect of Ardtornish. Owen and Emmeline Hugh Smith, who bought the estate in 1930, received yearly presents of named and un-named hybrids from Sir John Stirling Maxwell, of Pollok House, Glasgow.

To the east of the gardens, an estate road leads past Achranich, by the banks of the River Rannoch, out into the hills; climbing steeply through ancient woodlands, where the river charges down a long series of falls and white-churned pools.

At the top of the hill, the trees give way to a wide, moorland strath, enclosed southwards by Glais Bhein and "The Table of Lorn", a long, dark ridge, guarding Coire Slaghaig.

The going is easy along a well-defined track, which cuts through the mountains of Morvern into Kingairloch, reaching the sea by the old ruined castle of Glensanda on the shores of Loch Linnie.

Along the way, the track passes some excellent hill lochs where brown trout abound, including delightful Loch Tearnait, surely one of the most attractive waters in all of Scotland.

All the standard pattern Scottish loch flies will produce results on the Ardtornish Estate waters. My personal choice would be: Black Pennel, Ke-He, Soldier Palmer, Greenwell's Glory, March Brown, Wood cock & Hare Lug and Butchers; dressed on siz 14 hooks, fished three flies on a cast some twelve feet in length.

Dr. Macleod was right: "Get up and come along!" I can think of few other holiday locations which offer so much of interest for all the tribe - anglers and non-anglers alike.

FLY-FISHING - TEACHING THE YOUNGSTERS

by Lesley Crawford

Angling instruction with some youngsters on the Halladale Estuary.

If we, as adults, are keen anglers ourselves then more often than not, we are going to try to teach our offspring some of the joys of fly fishing. Ideally this should be an enjoyable exercise but it is perhaps more easy to lose your way, your patience and your dignity than you might think! Keep uppermost in your own mind at all times why you go fishing. The answer should be it's fun, it's relaxing, it's challenging and it's something different. Try and convey this to the youngster rather than deluging him in facts and the 'science' of fishing -

that will come in later life. Children's attention spans are short and when feet are twitching ready for the 'off' resist trying to 'lecture' at any great length. The good angler learns from his mistakes and practical experiences, not from 'text-book' reading, and he will continue to learn throughout his angling lifetime.

Having said that, as a SANA fly fishing instructor, I proffer up the following simple guidelines which I have found helpful in the past. Firstly take a really good picnic! This may sound a bit eccentric, but remember there are so many variables in fishing that are outwith your control, like the weather, the gales, the time of day, the hatch of fly and so on. Even if the youngster quickly masters the skill of casting he may still go home 'fishless' simply because it's too bright, cold, windy etc...! So take lots of favourite 'junk' food like crisps and Mars bars and your prospective audience will be that much more receptive! Next, see that they are properly equipped before you go and this includes as much, warm waterproof clothing, wellies and glasses for the eyes as it does the right rod and tackle. With such a bewildering array of tackle on the market these days plump for something light and relatively cheap first. You may find after all, that the obsession you have within you has not been passed into your child's genes and he may quickly confine an expensive rod to the broom cupboard either that or accidently stand on it! A light carbon based or fibre glass rod, 8 - 9 ft in length, light reel, floating line, 4 - 6 lb nylon and a few wet flies are all he or she is going to need. Small arms get tired easily so do not overload them with unwieldy equipment. Floating lines remember, though the water may actually merit a sinking one, are much easier to lift off the water and the ideal learners' tool. If you attach nylon to line and fly, and assemble all the equipment for their first outing by the water, all to the good. Small children are desperate to 'get going' and having to stand and watch you tie up knots in a gale does not encourage them! Indeed showing them any knots is better done away from the water at home when time and weather are not against you. Do bear in mind too the youngsters' previous fishing experiences for though they may never have fly fished they may well have caught something off a pier in the sea or with a worm in a stream or burn. That will all have helped bolster their confidence and re-assured them that fish are at least CATCHABLE and not mystical objects never seen or heard! It has been said by many anglers far greater than I in the past, that angling success has as much to do with confidence as it does with skill, so anything that you can do to encourage in general terms will help when the challenge of fly fishing presents itself. I am not so much of a purist as to suggest a six year old MUST learn fly fishing first, as sea fishing and trundling a worm down a burn is how I started!

Next, the actual business of CASTING begins. For a right hander a wind over the left shoulder is usually best as it keeps the fly away from the face. Note that a wind directly from behind is not recommended as it brings the fly of a beginner, back towards their neck or jacket! First put on a piece of wool or a fly without a hook so that the novice can see where it's going and what it's doing without injury. There are many lengthy tomes written on casting technique but remember the most elegant casters do not necessarily catch the most fish. Casting is only one part of fishing and it should not become an art in itself. It is simply a means of putting the fly out on the water to catch the fish. From experience I find the simplest way of teaching, is to keep using the words "Throw the line UP" - stop the rod at 12 o'clock - PAUSE - "throw the line OUT". These words are very carefully chosen as children's interpretation of what you say can be very literal. If you say something like the line goes 'back', it will, straight on to the ground behind, and if you say it comes 'down' it will, with an almighty crash!

Once they have a rudimentary idea of casting (learning spans will differ), put them over some trout, preferably free rising, suicidal ones! For that reason choose a venue where you know there are lots of 'easily' caught fish, if you have such a place nearby! Keep the interest going. Talk about what they are fishing for, what the fly is doing (representing a small insect, fish etc) and why, where the fish are likely to be, the influence of the weather and so on and give them plenty of BREAKS. This is where the good picnic comes in! Keep things relaxed and free and easy. If they want to stop and explore the shoreline then let them - they have a lifetime to learn after all. Remember, if you can, what you enjoyed as a child, a variety of things to do was without doubt very important! One of the greatest difficulties I have found is in fulfilling the child's expectations as, having learned basic casting, he will almost immediately expect to catch a fish! Of course as an experienced angler you may know it's just 'not on' for that day or that they have scared away every trout in sight! If so let him down gently while hopefully building on his knowledge of watercraft for, if he perseveres, finally that great day will dawn and he catches his first trout. A wise ghillie, hardened to many years of fishing and many types of anglers, once said to me he still gets an immense thrill from the beam of joy on a youngster's face when he catches his first fish. It's a moment of fantastic excitement and I'm very much in agreement with him. Catch one fish and confidence will grow and another convert will be made.

So keep it light, keep it interesting and do not be condescending, for they might end up showing you a thing or two when older! "Fishing is fun" is my teaching logo and if you can try and make it so for your youngsters you may well find they become well and truly 'hooked' for life.

DRY FLY FOR SCOTTISH TROUT

by Alan Spence

Here in the Borders and doubtless upon other large lowland rivers the past three decades have brought a transformation to the trout angling scene. This, the adoption of dry fly by many anglers, has overturned the once firm belief that for every trout taken by dry fly, the basket could be increased many fold by the use of wet fly tactics.

Both methods have of course the same end in the intention to deceive trout that a few wisps of fur and feather, held by silk upon a steel hook, is a natural insect in or on the waters of river or loch. Speaking of the Tweed and its tributaries, until the 1960's the majority of anglers opted for the wet fly. Not that this was exclusive as even then there were devotees to the floating or dry fly.

Traditional wet flies are mostly considered to represent a natural aquatic nymph as it rises towards the surface to transform there, 'hatch' in anglers' terms, into a winged insect. On the other hand it is possible that trout take the anglers' wet fly as the adult insect drowned in a heavy stream. Again the wet fly might represent a spinner, the final stage of all upwinged flies as it lies dead or dying on or near the surface.

Early season, April and the first two weeks in May, can see the wet fly reign supreme on stream and river. Come mid-May and the situation is reversed with the best results obtained by dry fly fishing. This is especially so once the evening rise gets underway when the floating fly, pert on stiff cock hackles upon the surface, is the required medicine.

The trend to dry fly fishing as summer approaches is no fad of the purist, simply it is on many waters becoming increasingly difficult to capture trout on wet fly during normal summer water levels. Why this should be so is difficult to determine but is perhaps due in some part to the increased amount of bottom, as opposed to underwater feeding now available to trout on the lower reaches of some rivers.

Trout taken in the evening on dry fly, surface feeders, are often packed with delicacies such as snails and caddis larvae, both bottom dwellers. Often the point of the jaw and the nose of these trout show abrasions from feeding on the bottom, indicating a preoccupation during daylight hours in this practice.

Yet as the light fails and the direct sunlight leaves the water these trout switch to surface feeding and for a brief spell can provide exciting sport. The trigger appears to be the arrival of flies on the surface, a hatch in other words, although occasional trout may be seen sipping at spinner from early evening.

Speaking here of Tweed, the deep salmon pools or dubs as they are called, harbour some first class trout. Trout whose weight can only be guessed at but possibly in the region of from four to five pounds. Veterans, well versed in the ways of the wiliest anglers, confidently rise beyond casting of all but the most proficient. Ever wary, the first ripple from the cautious angler entering the water will bring an abrupt end to feeding activity.

In the past dry fly fishing carried with it some mystique, born perhaps on the chalk streams of southern England. Chalk streams, where to fish anything other than a winged artificial dry fly, an exact imitation of the insect being taken by trout at the time, cast upstream to a rising trout was thought equal to the eighth sin of mankind. Much seems to have been made also of the difficulty of matching the natural insect, causing in the past many anglers to think that dry fly fishing was beyond their skills.

Today of course we know that this is not so. Anyone who is a moderately competent caster with reasonable eyesight is quite able to fish dry fly. For at least two reasons dry fly fishing is the easier method compared with any underwater method. First the surface disturbance, where a trout takes a fly, indicates immediately where the trout is feeding. Observation by the angler can reveal upon what natural fly the trout are taking, making the selection of an appropriate artificial much easier.

Occasionally on our Scottish rivers it can be a frustrating job trying to match an artificial fly to the natural being taken by the trout. This is especially the case when several different species of fly, in different stages of development, are on the water simultaneously. Hatching fly, adult and spinner, can all be present with a further problem in the fact that it is not always the largest most obvious flies which are being taken.

Most times it is easier, with a few fail-me-never patterns, in three sizes sufficient for 90 percent of occasions. For the remaining 10 it may be a desperate scramble through the fly box before an acceptable artificial is found.

Already mentioned is the classic method of dry fly presentation, the cast from below directly upstream to the trout's position. On small waters which can be covered from the bank this remains the best method with

Your trout sir, a 1½lb plus trout from a stream early evening.

the angler below and hopefully unseen by the trout. The strike in this instance has a much better chance of securing a hook hold pulling the hook directly into the jaw.

On Tweed tributaries such as the Whiteadder, and its feeder streams, the dry fly cast up into broken streamy water can provoke reaction from trout not actually seen to be rising. This is especially so in spring when fly hatches are spasmodic with fish eager to take every opportunity of a meal.

On the broad deep pools of large rivers such as the lower Tweed to be restricted to an upstream cast would leave many trout uncovered. It is perhaps the physical configuration of many of these pools which cause the angler to adopt a different approach.

Many of the best pools for dry fly fishing on the lower Tweed follow a pattern of alternate haughs and steep banks from side to side. From the haugh side shelving gravel makes easy wading and casting. Disturbance by the angler entering the water, especially when the river is at summer level, eliminates this approach to some degree.

On the steep bank side, usually closely backed by trees and bushes, deeper water is usually found where it is possible to fish from the bank or shallow ledges. It is here that the best dry fly fishing is usually to be found, not always easy but the rewards can outshine the difficulties.

Deep water and restricted wading prevent upstream casting, bringing an additional problem in the shape of drag to the angler who must cast across stream to cover his fish. Drag is the term applied to the flow of water acting on the line, causing the fly in turn, to move across the water at an unnatural direction and speed.

The cast from below a rising trout is less affected by drag but is to be expected when casting across stream. Some prevention can be attained by causing the line to land in a wriggle across the surface.

Stopping the rod as the line is about to land on the surface or pulling the rod slightly back at the same time achieves this effect. As the current pulls on the line, first the wriggles will straighten out, before a downstream belly occurs with accompanying drag, the fly will hopefully have passed over the trout's lie with either deception or refusal taking place.

Dry fly fishing on a large salmon pool on lower Tweed

Having said that, there are times when the dragging fly will induce a take, especially if trout are feeding on hatching sedge flies. Or a steadily rising fish persistently refusing the artificial may turn round and seize the fly if the line is given a gentle pull, twitching or dragging the fly for a few inches as it passes over its lie.

Trout feeding on surface flies usually occupy a position in the river, swimming forward and up to seize natural insects as they pass overhead, dropping back downstream to their original positions after each rise. These will be flies which come within their sphere of vision and depending on what depth the fish are lying at, may be between one and two feet either side.

At other times a fish may work its way upstream rising, dipping down then rising again several times before returning downstream to resume its beat. When small flies such as caneis, the fisherman's curse, are the target the pattern may be random with trout apparently circling sub surface as the fancy takes them.

Then there is the trout which feeds in a position say below an overhanging tree or in deep water which cannot be reached from below or across the stream. Difficult blighters, but the fly trotted down from above can prove their undoing, plenty of slack line cast from above with an inch or two fed through the rod rings as the fly crosses the lie. Not easy to set the hook from above but on occasions it does work and can prove the undoing of an otherwise inaccessible fish.

When does one fish dry fly? Whenever trout are rising is the easy answer with perhaps the cream of sport coming during summer spate conditions. Yes, brown coloured water in mid summer is a bonus for dry fly fishing, even if it is not an obvious time when trout are to be expected on the surface.

Summer spates after a long dry spell are dirty affairs washing accumulated tar and oil from roads and a cocktail of chemicals from agricultural land. An isolated spate in summer is often taboo as the river rises, but once peaked and beginning to fall some of the best fly hatches and trout rises of the year can be expected.

Even with four feet in the river and dirty brown the stimulus of fresh water is felt by insect, trout and angler. Now is the time to seek out any eddies or areas sheltered from the main flow, when conditions are right, action is assured. Dry fly fishing can in fact continue right through the stages of clearing water once beloved by the wet fly fisherman until the river regains normal summer level.

Large trout, denzies of the pool usually found lurking in mid-stream are now within casting range. Taking into account of course the steep tree-lined banks mentioned earlier

the foiler of many a perfect backcast. In spate conditions trout rise earlier in the evening and if anything the trout are less fussy on the exact pattern of artificial fly presented.

To put an exact formula on when to strike a trout taking a dry fly is difficult. There is no proper time as much depends upon exactly how the trout takes, which in turn is governed by what it is feeding on.

Experience alone tells, the slow sip at a spinner trapped in the surface film might require a few seconds pause before lifting the rod. The confident take of a hatching olive on a warm still evening a second only, while the quicksilver trout of the fast stream an instant response.

Fishing the slow running dubs in low water conditions requires fine tackle if trout are to be deceived. Drennan double strength in 4lbs breaking strain is claimed by its makers to have, at .148mm, a diameter equivalent to other brands of 2.6lbs breaking strain. Whatever diameter of nylon is used it is inadvisable to go below 3lbs b.s. when weed beds abound in summer. Leader points should always be degreased before starting fishing, floating leader points even in thin nylon, act as a warning beacon to trout on the surface of a slow running pool.

When dropping down to smaller sizes of hook such as 18 and 20, my own faith is pinned on the Partridge Captain Hamilton down eyed dry fly hooks, a reliable hook where strength is concerned and also, despite the small size, holds exceptionally well.

A tapered leader is handy, keeping the bulky fly line well clear of fish. This should be stepped down to the fine point with progressive 5lb and 4lb b.s. by four turn water knots. The line, a double tapered floater, although where backcasting is restricted a forward taper would be an advantage were it not for the less delicate presentation these lines make.

Using fine tackle with a powerful rod would be futile; a rating from 6 downwards not too stiff in the action would be adequate. Length; a matter of preference 7 - 9 ft for small rivers and up to 11 ft for better line control on larger.

On lochs also, more anglers are now willing to adopt dry fly tactics which were previously reserved for doldrums conditions of flat calm and bright sunlight. River dry fly fishing is a rapid fire affair of cast, cover fish, recover fly, false cast to dry fly before recasting every five or ten seconds. On lochs it can assume a leisurely pace casting to the edge of a ripple being patrolled by a surface feeding fish.

On lochs, trout have a much better opportunity to seize the ascending nymph of aquatic hatching insects making it the case that overall they perhaps feed rather less on the adult fly on the surface. This does not mean that trout do not take the angler's representation of the adult fly fished dry. In fact for the stillwater angler a combination of floating and sub surface flies can be adopted giving the best of both worlds.

Some of the most exciting sport on lochs can be had when terrestrial flies are blown on the water. This can occur throughout the angling season but a fall of land insects is most likely between late April and September. Of most use to the angler are black gnats, hawthorn flies, crane flies or daddy long legs, heather flies in autumn and throughout the season the rather dis-gusting cow dung fly.

Daddy long legs provide a meaty morsel and can bring to the surface some of the better quality trout in any stillwater. Nerve-tingling stuff it can be, awaiting the swirl of a large trout to come within casting range. Then that agonising moment after the artificial fly disappears, or is sunk by a flick of the trout's tail to be sampled underwater, waiting for line to draw tight confirming that the fish has indeed taken the offering.

Whether dry fly trout fishing is practised on river or loch it represents one of the most exciting of all forms of trout angling, stalking and casting to a fish actually seen to be feeding.

Prime summer trout taken on dry fly.

GAME ANGLING CLUBS

CLUB	SECRETARY
Aberfeldy Angling Club	S.B. Richardson, 14 Farragon Drive, Aberfeldy, Perthshire PH15 2BQ. Tel: (0887) 20024
Airdrie Angling Club	Roy Burgess, 21 Elswick Drive, Caldercruix.
Annan & District Angling Club	J. Glen, 110 High Street, Annan, Dumfriesshire.
Badenoch Angling Association	J. Dallas, The Mills, Kingussie.
Berwick & District Angling Association	D. Cowan, 3 Church Street, Berwick. Tel: (0289) 330145.
Blairgowrie, Rattray & District Angling Association	W. Matthew, 4 Mitchell Square, Blairgowrie, Perthshire. Tel: (0250) 3679.
Brechin Angling Club	D.E. Smith, 3 Friendly Park, Brechin, Angus.
Castle Douglas & District Angling Association	Ian Bendall, Tommy's Sports Shop, Castle Douglas, Kirkcudbrightshire. Tel: (0556) 2851.
Chatton Angling Association	A. Jarvis, 7 New Road, Alnwick.
Coldstream & District Angling Association	H.F. Bell, 12 Priory Hill, Coldstream, Berwickshire TD12 4RE. Tel: (0890) 2171.
Cramond Angling Club	D. Wilkie, 37 Craigs Road, Edinburgh EH12 3EW. Tel: 031-339 1801.
Dalbeattie Angling Association	G.W. Garroch, 15 Church Street, Dalbeattie DG5 4BA. Tel: (0556) 611373.
Devon Angling Association	R. Breingan, 33 Redwell Place, Alloa.
Dreghorn Angling Club	Dr. D.D. Muir, 6 Pladda Avenue, Broomlands, Irvine.
Dumfries & Galloway Angling Association	D. Byers, 4 Bloomfield, Edinburgh Road, Dumfries DG1 1SG. Tel: (0387) 53850.
Dunkeld & Birnam Angling Association	J. Doig, 42 Willowbank, Dunkeld, Perthshire PH8 0JU. Tel: 612.
Dunoon & District Angling Club	D.& D.A.C., 7 Blair Lane, Stewart Street, Dunoon. Tel: Dunoon 5732.

CLUB	SECRETARY
Earlston Angling Association	P. Hessett, 2 Arnot Place, Earlston. Tel: 577.
Eckford Angling Association	R.B. Anderson, W.S., Royal Bank Buildings, Jedburgh, Roxburghshire. Tel: 3202.
Elgin & District Angling Association	Mr. F. Rhind, "Birchview", Wester Whitewreath, Longmorn, Elgin, Morayshire.
Esk & Liddle Fisheries Association	R.J.B. Hill, Solicitor, Bank of Scotland Buildings, Langholm, Dumfriesshire.
Esk Valley Angling Improvement Association	Kevin Burns, 53 Fernieside Crescent, Edinburgh.
Eye Water Angling Club	W.S. Gillie, 2 Tod's Court, Eyemouth, Berwickshire
Ford & Etal Estates Fishing Club	Mr. W.M. Bell, Heatherslaw, Cornhill on Tweed. Tel: Crookham 221.
Fyvie Angling Association	J.D. Pirie, Prenton, South Road, Oldmeldrum, Aberdeenshire AB5 0AB.
Gordon Fishing Club	Mrs. M. Forsyth, 47 Main Street, Gordon. Tel: 359.
Greenlaw Angling Club	J. Purves, 9 Wester Row, Greenlaw.
Hawick Angling Club	R. Sutherland, 20 Longhope Drive, Hawick. Tel: 75150.
Inverness Angling Club	G.M. Smith, 50 Nevis Park, Inverness.
Irvine & District Angling Club	A. Sim, 51 Rubie Crescent, Irvine.
Jedforest Angling Club	J.T. Renilson, 4 Canongate, Jedburgh, Roxburghshire.
Kelso Angling Association	R. Yule, 6 High Croft, Kelso, Roxburghshire. Tel: 23907.
Killin, Breadalbane Angling Club	Douglas Allan, 12 Ballechroisk, Killin. Tel: (05672) 362.
Kilmaurs Angling Club	J. Watson, 7 Four Acres Drive, Kilmaurs.

CLUB	SECRETARY	CLUB	SECRETARY
Kintyre Fish Protection & Angling Club	F.W. Neate, Kilmoray Place, High St, Campbeltown.	Peebleshire Salmon Fishing Association	Blackwood & Smith W.S., 39 High Street, Peebles.
Kyles of Bute Angling Club	R. Newton, Viewfield Cottage, Tighnabruaich, Argyll.	Perth & District Anglers' Association	G. Nichols, 30 Wallace Crescent, Perth.
		Pitlochry Angling Club	R. Harriman, Sunnyknowe, Nursing Home Brae, Pitlochry. Tel: (0796) 2484.
Ladykirk & Norham Angling Association	Mr. R.G. Wharton, 8 St. Cuthbert's Square, Norham. Tel: (0289) 82467.	Rannoch & District Angling Club	J. Brown, Esq., The Square, Kinloch Rannoch, Tayside. Tel: Kinloch Rannoch 268.
Lairg Angling Club	J.M. Ross, St. Murie, Church Hill Road, Lairg, Sutherland IV27 4BL. Tel: Lairg 2010.	River Almond Angling Association	H. Meikle, 23 Glen Terrace, Deans, Livingston.
Larbert & Stenhousemuir Angling Club	A. Paterson, 6 Wheatlands Avenue, Bonnybridge, Stirlingshire.	St. Andrews Angling Club	Secretary, 54 St. Nicholas Street, St. Andrews. Tel: (0334) 76347.
Lauderdale Angling Association	D.M. Milligan, 1 Newbyth Stables, East Linton, East Lothian.	St. Marys Loch Angling Club	Mr. J. Miller, 8/5 Craighouse Gardens, Edinburgh. Tel: 031-447 0024.
Lochgilphead & District Angling Club	H. McArthur, The Tackle Shop, Lochnell Street, Lochgilphead.	Stanley & District Angling Club	D.J. Jeffrey, Airntully, Stanley. Tel: Stanley 463.
Loch Keose Angling Association	c/o Tourist Information Centre, Stornoway, Lewis.	Selkirk & District Angling Association	Mr. A. Murray, 40 Raeburn Meadows, Selkirk. Tel: 21534.
Loch Lomond Angling Improvement Association	R.A. Clements, C.A., 224 Ingram Street, Glasgow.	Stormont Angling Club	The Factor, Scone Estates Office, Scone Palace. Perth.
Loch Rannoch Conservation Association	Mrs. Steffen, Coilmore Cottage, Kinloch Rannoch.	Stranraer & District Angling Association	Ted Ainsworth, c/o Creach More Golf Club, Stranraer.
Melrose & District Angling Association	T. McLeish, Planetree Cottage, Newstead, Melrose. Tel: 2232.	Strathmore Angling Improvement Association	Mrs. A. Henderson, 364 Blackness Road, Dundee. Tel: Dundee 68062.
Morebattle Angling Club	Mr. H. Fox, Orchard Cottage, Morebattle.	Turriff Angling Association	Ian Masson, 6 Castle Street, Turriff, AB5 7BJ.
Murthly & Glendelvine Trout Angling Club	Chairman, A.M. Allan, Drummond Hall, Murthly, Perthshire.	Upper Annandale Angling Association	J. Black, 1 Rosehill, Grange Road, Moffat. Tel: Moffat 20104.
New Galloway Angling Association	N. Birch, Galloway View, Balmaclellan, Castle Douglas. Tel: New Galloway 404.	Upper Nithsdale Angling Club	W. Forsyth, Solicitor, 100 High Street, Sanquhar, Dumfriesshire. Tel: Sanquhar 50241.
North Uist Angling Club	Factor, North Uist Estate, Estate Office, Lochmaddy, North Uist.	Whiteadder Angling Association	R. Baker, Millburn House, Duns. Tel: Duns 83086.
Peebleshire Trout Fishing Association	D.G. Fyfe, 39 High Street, Peebles. Tel: 20131.		

CLOSE SEASON

The following are the statutory close season dates for trout and salmon fishing in Scotland.

TROUT

The close season for trout in Scotland is from 7 October to 14 March, both days inclusive, but many clubs extend this close season still further to allow the fish to reach better condition.

Fresh trout may not be sold between the end of August and the beginning of April, and not at any time if less than eight inches long.

SALMON

Net Fishing	Rod Fishing	River District
1 Sept-15 Feb	1 Nov-15 Feb	Add
27 Aug-10 Feb	1 Nov-10 Feb	Ailort
27 Aug-10 Feb	1 Nov-10 Feb	Aline
27 Aug-10 Feb	1 Nov-10 Feb	Alness
27 Aug-10 Feb	1 Nov-10 Feb	Applecross
27 Aug-10 Feb	1 Nov-10 Feb	Arnisdale (Loch Hourn)
27 Aug-10 Feb	16 Oct-10 Feb	Awe
27 Aug-10 Feb	1 Nov-10 Feb	Ayr
27 Aug-10 Feb	1 Nov-10 Feb	Baa & Goladoir
27 Aug-10 Feb	1 Nov-10 Feb	Badachro & Kerry (Gairloch)
27 Aug-10 Feb	1 Nov-10 Feb	Balgay & Shieldaig
27 Aug-10 Feb	16 Oct-10 Feb	Beauly
27 Aug-10 Feb	1 Nov-10 Feb	Berriedale
10 Sept-24 Feb	1 Nov-24 Feb	Bervie
27 Aug-10 Feb	1 Nov-10 Feb	Bladenoch
27 Aug-10 Feb	1 Nov-10 Feb	Broom
27 Aug-10 Feb	16 Oct-31 Jan	Brora
10 Sept-24 Feb	1 Nov-24 Feb	Carradale
27 Aug-10 Feb	1 Nov-10 Feb	Carron (W. Ross)
10 Sept-24 Feb	1 Nov-24 Feb	Clayburn (Isle of Harris (East))
27 Aug-10 Feb	1 Nov-10 Feb	Clyde & Leven
27 Aug-10 Feb	1 Oct-25 Jan	Conon
14 Sept-28 Feb	15 Oct-28 Feb	Cree
27 Aug-10 Feb	17 Oct-10 Feb	Creed or Stornoway and Laxay (Isle of Lewis)
27 Aug-10 Feb	1 Nov-10 Feb	Creran (Loch Creran)
27 Aug-10 Feb	1 Nov-10 Feb	Croe & Shiel
27 Aug-10 Feb	1 Oct-31 Jan	Dee (Aberdeenshire)
27 Aug-10 Feb	1 Nov-10 Feb	Dee (Kirkcudbrightshire)
27 Aug-10 Feb	1 Nov-10 Feb	Deveron
27 Aug-10 Feb	1 Nov-10 Feb	Don
27 Aug-10 Feb	1 Nov-10 Feb	Doon
1 Sept-15 Feb	16 Oct-15 Feb	Drummachloy or Glenmore (Isle of Bute)
27 Aug-10 Feb	16 Oct-10 Feb	Dunbeath
21 Aug- 4 Feb	1 Nov-31 Jan	Earn
1 Sept-15 Feb	1 Nov-15 Feb	Echaig
1 Sept-15 Feb	1 Nov-15 Feb	Esk, North
1 Sept-15 Feb	1 Nov-15 Feb	Esk, South
27 Aug-10 Feb	1 Nov-10 Feb	Ewe (Isle of Harris (West))
27 Aug-10 Feb	6 Oct-10 Feb	Findhorn
10 Sept-24 Feb	1 Nov-24 Feb	Fleet (Kirkcudbright)
10 Sept-24 Feb	1 Nov-24 Feb	Fleet (Sutherland)
27 Aug-10 Feb	1 Nov-10 Feb	Forss
27 Aug-10 Feb	1 Nov-31 Jan	Forth
1 Sept-15 Feb	1 Nov-15 Feb	Fyne, Shira & Aray (Loch Fyne)
10 Sept-24 Feb	1 Nov-24 Feb	Girvan
27 Aug-10 Feb	1 Nov-10 Feb	Glenelg
27 Aug-10 Feb	1 Nov-10 Feb	Gour
27 Aug-10 Feb	1 Nov-10 Feb	Greiss, Laxdale or Thunga
27 Aug-10 Feb	1 Nov-10 Feb	Grudie or Dionard
27 Aug-10 Feb	1 Nov-10 Feb	Gruinard and Little Gruinard
27 Aug-10 Feb	1 Oct-11 Jan	Halladale, Strathy, Naver & Borgie
27 Aug-10 Feb	1 Oct-10 Jan	Helmsdale
27 Aug-10 Feb	1 Oct-11 Jan	Hope and Polla or Strathbeg
10 Sept-24 Feb	1 Nov-24 Feb	Howmore
27 Aug-10 Feb	1 Nov-10 Feb	Inchard
10 Sept-24 Feb	1 Nov-24 Feb	Inner (on Jura)
27 Aug-10 Feb	1 Nov-10 Feb	Inver
10 Sept-24 Feb	1 Nov-24 Feb	Iora (on Arran)
10 Sept-24 Feb	1 Nov-24 Feb	Irvine & Garnock
27 Aug-10 Feb	1 Nov-10 Feb	Kannaird
27 Aug-10 Feb	1 Nov-10 Feb	Kilchoan
27 Aug-10 Feb	1 Nov-10 Feb	Kinloch (Kyle of Tongue)
27 Aug-10 Feb	1 Nov-10 Feb	Kirkaig
27 Aug-10 Feb	1 Nov-10 Feb	Kishorn
27 Aug-10 Feb	1 Oct-10 Jan	Kyle of Sutherland
10 Sept-24 Feb	1 Nov-10 Feb	Laggan & Sorn (Isle of Islay)
27 Aug-10 Feb	1 Nov-10 Feb	Laxford

Net Fishing	Rod Fishing	River District	Net Fishing	Rod Fishing	River District
27 Aug-10 Feb	1 Nov-10 Feb	Little Loch Broom	27 Aug-10 Feb	1 Nov-10 Feb	Pennygowan or
27 Aug-10 Feb	1 Nov-10 Feb	Loch Duich			Glenforsa & Aros
27 Aug-10 Feb	1 Nov-10 Feb	Loch Luing			
27 Aug-10 Feb	17 Oct-10 Feb	Loch Roag	27 Aug-10 Feb	1 Nov-10 Feb	Resort
27 Aug-10 Feb	1 Nov-10 Feb	Lochy	1 Sept-15 Feb	1 Nov-15 Feb	Ruel
27 Aug-10 Feb	16 Oct-10 Feb	Lossie			
10 Sept-24 Feb	1 Nov-24 Feb	Luce	27 Aug-10 Feb	1 Nov-10 Feb	Sanda
27 Aug-10 Feb	1 Nov-10 Feb	Lussa	27 Aug-10 Feb	1 Nov-10 Feb	Scaddle
		(Isle of Mull)	10 Sept-24 Feb	1 Nov-24 Feb	Shetland Isles
			27 Aug-10 Feb	1 Nov-10 Feb	Shiel
27 Aug-10 Feb	1 Nov-10 Feb	Moidart	27 Aug-10 Feb	1 Nov-10 Feb	Sligachan
27 Aug-10 Feb	1 Nov-10 Feb	Morar	27 Aug-10 Feb	1 Nov-10 Feb	Snizort
20 Sept-24 Feb	1 Nov-24 Feb	Mullangaren,	27 Aug-10 Feb	1 Oct-10 Feb	Spey
		Horasary and	10 Sept-24 Feb	1 Nov-24 Feb	Stinchar
		Lochnaciste	27 Aug-10 Feb	1 Nov-10 Feb	Sunart
		(Isle of North Uist)			(except Earn)
			21 Aug- 4 Feb	16 Oct-14 Jan	Tay
27 Aug-10 Feb	1 Oct-10 Feb	Nairn	27 Aug-10 Feb	6 Oct-10 Jan	Thurso
27 Aug-10 Feb	1 Nov-10 Feb	Nell, Feochan	27 Aug-10 Feb	1 Nov-10 Feb	Torridon
		and Euchar	15 Sept-14 Feb	1 Dec-31 Jan	Tweed
27 Aug-10 Feb	16 Oct-14 Jan	Ness			
10 Sept-24 Feb	1 Dec-24 Feb	Nith	10 Sept-24 Feb	1 Nov- 9 Feb	Ugie
			27 Aug-10 Feb	1 Nov-10 Feb	Ullapool
10 Sept-24 Feb	1 Nov-24 Feb	Orkney Isles	10 Sept-24 Feb	1 Dec-24 Feb	Urr
27 Aug-10 Feb	1 Nov-10 Feb	Ormsary (Loch			
		Killisport), Loch	27 Aug-10 Feb	1 Nov-10 Feb	Wick
		Head & Stornoway			
			10 Sept-24 Feb	1 Nov-10 Feb	Ythan

There is no close season for coarse fishing.

THE FORTH FISHERY CONSERVATION TRUST

The Trust was formed in August 1987, with the aim of improving all the fisheries within the Forth catchment area which extends from Fifeness to Balquidder in the north, and Loch Katrine to Torness in the south. The initial aim was to purchase a boat to assist the Forth District Salmon Fishery Board stop illegal netting of salmon on the Estuary.

Within twelve weeks two 18ft high speed launches were acquired for use by the new Superintendent Water Bailiff, Ian Baird, and the impact on the illegal netting operations has been dramatic. The River Teith and its tributaries experienced a good run of spring salmon and sea trout are running through almost unhindered.

The Trust has also stimulated discussions on salmon poaching and fish conservation at the hghest legal and government levels and will continue that dialogue.

Although a number of enthusiastic clubs have worked hard to open up fisheries, to restock and protect them, the Forth catchment area remains a virtually untapped fishery. These could be developed to provide leisure, tourism and employment for the region.

There are three major tasks the Trust wishes to undertake.

1. To increase efforts to eliminate all illegal fishing both on the estuary and throughout the whole river system.
2. To identify ownership of all stretches of water and fisheries in the area so that more effective supervision may be introduced.
3. To review the existing population and habitat of all fish species and assess the potential for increasing their numbers throughout the area.

This information will help all clubs, landowners and local inhabitants to make the best possible use of available resources and improve the quality of salmon, sea trout and coarse fishing throughout the Forth catchment area.

SCOTTISH FRESHWATER FISH RECORDS

Bream   5 lb 15 oz. 12 dr = 2.714 kg. Castle Loch, Dumfriesshire. H. Wood, 1973.

Carp   26 lb 2oz. Saul Killeen, Duddingston Loch, 1990.

Dace   1 lb 3oz. 8 dr. = 0.55 kg. River Tweed, Coldstream, G. Keech, 1979.

Eel   5 lb 8 oz. = 2.495 kg, Loch Ochiltree, T. May, 1987.

Goldfish   1 lb 9 oz. = 0.709 kg, Forth & Clyde Canal, B. Stevenson, 1978.

Grayling   2 lb 14 oz. 2 dr. = 0.709 kg, Lyne Water, R. Brown, 1987.

Perch   4 lb 14 oz. Joe Walker, Loch Ard, 1989.

Pike   47 lb 11 oz. = 21.631 kg, Loch Lomond, Tom Morgan, 1947.

Roach   3 lb 2½ oz. Danny O'Rourke, Strathclyde Park 1990.

Tench   4 lb 14 oz. = 2.211 kg, Spectacle Loch, B. Gilbert, 1983.

No records exist for the following species. Claims can be made over the qualifying weights:

Barbel	1 lb.	**Gudgeon**	4 oz.
Bleak	2 oz.	**Rudd**	2 lb.
Cat Fish	1 lb.	**Ruffe**	4 oz.
Chub	2 lb.	**Silver Bream**	8 oz.
Crucian Carp	2 lb.	**Zander**	1 lb.
Golden Orfe	2 lb.		

How to claim a record:

1. No claims will be considered for dead fish. All fish must be returned to the water alive.

2. The claim should be made on a form available from the Development Committee who must be satisfied by the evidence that the fish was correctly identified and weighed, and was captured by fair angling.

3. New claims will be considered subject to the following minimum requirements:
a) Photographs of the fish must be available.
b) The scales must be certified as being accurate.
c) Witnesses will assist the claim and if possible these should be experienced anglers.

SCOTTISH FEDERATION FOR COARSE ANGLING

The Federation was formed in 1975 to promote and encourage the sport of Coarse Angling in Scotland. It is recognised by the Scottish Sports Council as being the governing body for Coarse Angling throughout Scotland.

Objects and Functions

To obtain waters for coarse angling.
To assist with fisheries management.
To assist with stocking of waters.
To promote and develop coarse angling in Scotland.
To promote and organise competitions and league matches.
To provide team representation at the World Championships (CIPS-FIPS-ED).
To organise international events for Scottish anglers.

Members

At present, seven clubs are affiliated to the Federation. Individual membership of the Federation is available although it is preferred that individuals join clubs affiliated to the Federation. The annual subscription for Club Membership of the SFCA is £25 with a joining fee of £12.50.
Individual membership is offered at £3.00

Coaching and Courses

Some SFCA member clubs hold 'in class' coaching sessions for novice anglers, while others operate 'on the bank' instruction thus providing knowledge under varying conditions.

Committee Structure

The affairs of the Federation are at present conducted by a Management Committee comprising the Chairman, Hon. Secretary, Hon Treasurer and Club representatives.
A development and a Match Angling Committee also exist to deal with specific projects.

Office Bearers

Chairman
Jim Carnie, 54 Watling Street, Uddingston, Nr. Glasgow.
Tel: Uddingston 817764.

Secretary
Jim Brown, 13 Boghead Road, Kirkintilloch, Nr. Glasgow.
Tel: 041-776 6741.

Treasurer
Tony Ball, 92 Westergreens Avenue, Kirkintilloch, Nr. Glasgow.
Tel: 041 775 2964.

Match Committee Chairman (Team Manager)
Alistair Keir, Tigh Na Fluers, M11 O Gryfe Road, Bridge of Weir, Renfrewshire.
Tel: Bridge of Weir 612580.

Match Committee Secretary
Dave Brampton.

Central Match Angling Club:
C. Palmer, 64 Dawson Place, Bo'ness.
Tel: Bo'ness 823953.

Edinburgh Angling Club:
Ron Woods, 23 Terragles, Penicuik.
Tel: (0968) 74792.

Forth and Clyde Coarse Angling Club:
P. Morrisey, 18 Daiglen. Tillicoultry, Clacks.
Tel: 0259 50757.

Glasgow Match Angling Club:
F. Hetherington, 4 Rosebery Place, Eliburn, Livingston.

Glasgow & West of Scotland Regional Association of the Pike Anglers Club of Great Britain:
Ralston MacPherson, 17 Barhill Court, Kirkintilloch.

Kirkintilloch Angling Club:
J. Brown, 13 Boghead Road, Kirkintilloch, Nr. Glasgow.
Tel: 041-776 6741.

Linlithgow Angling Club:
E. Gilbert, 12 Claredon Road, Linlithgow.
Tel. Linlithgow 845115.

Milton Angling Club:
D. Morrison, 112 Scaraway Street, Milton, Glasgow.

Strathclyde Angling Club:
Jim Byers, 16 Jade Terrace., Bellshill.

Competition
Summer and Winter Club Leagues are held each year. Overall results provide the Scottish Team and Individual champions. Scottish National Junior Open Championship.

All Scotland championship - Scottish residents only.

Scottish Federation Open.

Scottish Federation Cup - Federation members only.

Home International Series. International friendlies against other countries.

Participation in the World Championships.

Scottish Pole Angling Championship. Member clubs also arrange club match programmes throughout spring, summer and autumn.

Specimen Group
A newly formed and active element of the Federation. Objectives include: Providing an efficiently managed fishery befitting the Federation membership. Continually updating the 'Available Waters Register' for the benefits of all Scottish coarse anglers and visitors.

THE S.F.C.A. COARSE ANGLER'S COUNTRY CODE

1. Never throw away hooks, line or shot.
   Take them home and get rid of them properly.

2. Plastic bags can kill.
   Take away all rubbish from your spot,
   even if it was there before.

3. Know the fishery rules and return all coarse fish,
   including pike and eels, unharmed.

4. Help protect wildlife, plants and trees.
   Fish well away from birds' nesting places.

5. Place your keepnet to hold your fish properly.
   Stake it out if you can.

6. Use barbless hooks when you can.
   Take care when casting.

7. Park cars away from entrances.
   Keep to paths and close all gates.

8. Carbon rods conduct electricity.
   Keep well away from overhead power lines.

9. Don't light fires.
   Report any sign of pollution.

10. Keep dogs under control.
    Don't disturb the peace of the countryside.

DEFEND YOUR SPORT
JOIN THE SCOTTISH FEDERATION FOR COARSE ANGLING

NATURAL AND ARTIFICIAL
SEA ANGLING BAITS

by Alan Spence

Within Scottish waters swim fish whose weight may be anything from a few ounces to hundreds of pounds. Fish which will eat at one time or another anything which swims in, or crawls below, the sea. Despite this abundant larder, where small fish are eaten by larger fish which in turn may fall prey to even larger, there are times for the angler when only one specific bait will prove successful.

This is brought home to charter angling skippers when a few members of the party have a heavy bag at the end of the day, while the catch by others is only moderate or even poor. Setting aside the ability of individual anglers, on most occasions it is those who have gone to the trouble to gather fresh bait who have the greatest success.

But which bait, and most important what size of bait? A large predator would be unlikely to take a small bait while plaice or other flatfish would find it impossible to swallow the whole mackerel or coalfish aimed at tope or skate.

When boat fishing for what are considered table fish, codling and haddock for example, some baits are miles ahead of all others. League leaders could be considered mussel and lugworm, as fresh as possible. For the former the best results always seem to come when they are not only fresh but shelled aboard the boat.

Alive alive O, as that famous maiden from Dublin cried while wheeling her wares through the streets. So also for fish, shelling aboard seems to have a bonus in that the discarded shells provide a constant stream of water borne scent drawing fish towards the boat.

A snag with mussel is, that until expert, the art of shelling is a time consuming exercise which can waste precious minutes when sport is fast and furious. A soft bait also, which is easily removed from the hook by fish, so soft that it will gradually wash from the hook while fishing.

This is again perhaps one of the successes of mussel, the steady stream of particles washing downtide. Securing mussel on the hook can be best done with elasticated thread preventing leaching to some extent. Old hands used sheep's wool gathered from hedges, the theory being that this tangled fish's teeth making it impossible for them to eject the hook once taken.

Mussel has another advantage over other popular sea baits in that it freezes well, an ideal standby for inland sea anglers who do not have access to fresh bait. Frozen packs of mussels are next best and can usually be bought from fishmongers or supermarket freezer shelves.

The best mussel beds are found in sheltered Firths and sea lochs away from the force of heavy seas, usually on sandy mud or pure mud foreshores which dry out at half tide. It is a simple matter to collect a supply of the best specimens which can be kept alive for an indefinite period, stored in a mesh sack, and hung over the boat's side.

For general fishing there is little to separate the results from mussel and that other sea angler's and sea fish's favourite the lugworm. Fresh is always best, a box of lugworm exposed to heat and going 'off' soon advertises its own presence.

Some lugworm can be found on open storm beaches but usually these are few and of a poor size. Soft muddy sand is the most common habitat for lug which like mussel, are usually found on sheltered beaches.

Conveniently lugworm advertise their position by throwing up a cast, a curly coil of sand, while a short distance away a shallow dimple in the sand indicates its breathing hole. Somewhere in between lies the worm itself, spending its life filtering sand to extract the nourishment from the minute organisms within.

About the best tool for lug extraction is a broad tined fork such as gardeners use for potato digging, this having less chance of damaging or cutting through worms than a spade. Where casts are prolific, random digging forming a trench can, after some sweat, ensure a supply of bait, always remembering to back fill when digging is finished.

Where lug casts are fewer it may be a case of hunting individuals, almost as exciting as fishing itself. Look for the sand cast and hopefully its matching breathing hole digging carefully down from the cast end until the worm is found at the 'U' bend.

Retaining lugworm in fish catching condition depends upon how warm or cold conditions prevail coupled with proper storage. Damaged worms should not be stored along with prime specimens, these former will rapidly induce mass genocide in the whole stock. Longest live storage is best achieved by wrapping each specimen individually in newspaper, before packing in layers with more newspaper.

Second best is layers of newspaper with, if possible, the worms not touching each other, four or five worms only to a layer in a standard bucket. Dry sand is the third option keeping lugworm alive for much longer periods than wet, which should only be considered for short term storage, that is worms dug to be used the same day.

The above dry storage methods only work when the bait is kept cool, and certainly away from the direct rays of the sun, not always an easy matter for the holiday angler. Lug are less suitable for freezing, emerging as a limp watery mass but moderate refrigeration helps keep bait alive for a longer period.

Long term storage can be achieved by using a salt water aquarium. There is however some debate as to how attractive lugworm are to fish, after a week under these artificial conditions. Salting renders the lugworm hard and tough but again does not appeal to fish to the same extent as fresh.

Of the marine worms found in Scotland the second most important is the ragworm, growing to over 12 inches in length with a centipede like appearance and tweezer like jaws which can administer a fairly sharp nip. Large rag favour mud, especially where this is found among flat shale like stones. Some affinity is shared by the ragworm and mussel, the two species often being found on the same ground.

It is possible that in some areas there may be regulations governing digging in mussel beds which are exploited commercially, so it is worthwhile checking before commencing operations. Similarly many tidal harbours abound with large ragworm but digging is not encouraged or indeed may be prohibited entirely.

For boat owners the banning of digging in harbours is a sensible precaution, brought about mainly by damage caused to vessels in the past through careless bait gatherers leaving sharp stones and boulders liable to puncture and sink small boats. It is essential to stress that no matter where the sea angler digs bait, the beach or foreshore should be returned to its original condition.

Sea angling bait is now in such demand that at least one commercial ragworm farm, using surplus warm water from a power station to speed growth, is now in operation in north east England. These farmed worms are packed in insulated vermiculite chippings and can keep for up to a week in a domestic type refrigerator. Wild ragworm should be treated to the same storage conditions as lug, where if anything they are the less delicate of the two species.

The baits discussed so far are equally efficient be they intended for shore or boat angling. When it comes to the former many anglers will place before these, soft and peeler crab. Like all crustacea the green shore crab before it can grow, must cast or moult its present hard shell.

Prior to casting it is in what is known as the peeler stage, that is the new soft shell is formed below the soon to be discarded old. These are distinguished by it being possible to lift the rear flap slightly, or a segment of leg can be removed, revealing a new soft leg underneath.

Soft crabs are those which have already cast their shell being soft and jelly-like to touch. If this crab is a female it is most likely that a hard shelled male will be guarding her, as it is only when the female is in the soft state that mating can take place.

Rock pools and ledges are the haunt of green crab, often found below hanging curtains of seaweed, under rocks and stones, discarded tyres in fact anywhere where the crab can feel secure and hidden when at its most vulnerable. Usually in Scotland it is not until mid-May that the first peeler and soft crabs can be expected, with a peak in late June.

Peelers as indicated must have the hard shell removed, the legs can be peeled individually and baited over the hook point. Soft crabs only require insertion on the hook and like peeler they are best bound on with elasticated thread.

Fishing from rock edges during the summer months the green crab in soft or peeler stages is hard to beat, codling, pollack and coalfish all being willing takers. A first class bait for use by the inshore boat angler also, although oddly in its hard state the green crab is of little use as bait, despite the fact that fish are known to eat green crabs in their hard state.

Other natural baits which can be gathered from rock edges include hermit crabs, a first class bait this, whelks and limpets, this latter being a last resort. On beaches razorfish, cockles and clams can be found as are small white ragworm when digging on lug ground. These are less common baits than those dealt with earlier in detail but razorfish and clams can be on a par with mussel in sheer fish catching terms.

Earlier it was mentioned that fish eat smaller fish. It follows therefore that fish baits should be an effective means of securing a decent bag. Mackerel more than any other fish is used as bait for sea angling around Scotland, mainly from boats but it also has its place in shore angling.

Without doubt when conditions are right a bright shining strip from a mackerel's belly will form an attractive bait for many species of sea fish. This is especially so when fish are hunting shoals of sand eels or small herring, a usual habit during summer months when bait fish are plentiful.

All fish of the cod family can fall to a mackerel strip and here again fresh is the word, a mackerel caught the same day/hour/minute is vastly superior to yesterday's or even a frozen. Mackerel in some form or another can go right up the food chain as a bait.

Minute slips for flatfish, strips or lasks for cod etc rising up through fillets to a whole fish for common skate. Fortunately mackerel are easily captured using feather traces during the summer months when shoals are at their most dense. A few minutes work by the boat party should soon secure enough bait to begin more serious operations.

For shore fishing a mackerel head or fillet, free lined without any sinker, can prove the undoing of inshore conger in deep water. Pollack and large coalfish can also fall to mackerel strip fished around gullies and weed beds.

Occasionally when feathering for mackerel the greater sand eel is foul hooked. Like the mackerel this is an oily fleshed fish, strips cut from either side making an excellent bait for all round bottom fishing.

Oily fish such as mackerel, herring and sand eel tend to be soft when thawed after being deep frozen a factor which does not affect either octopus or squid. These baits are now available frozen from some tackle dealers and when cut into strips appropriate to the size of quarry are one of the best deep frozen baits the sea angler can use. These are also on sale in a preserved state but as such are less attractive to fish than fresh or frozen.

Whatever natural bait is chosen fish may at times be finicky and most sea anglers will be familiar with the occasions when fish bite but are not hooked. Or they may be only lightly held, to be lost when playing or near the surface. Sometimes these shy feeders can be overcome by changing to a smaller hook only lightly baited, which seems to be taken more readily in these circumstances.

A natural bait is not always essential for sea angling success particularly where boat angling is concerned. Artificial lures have their proper place when fish feeding patterns suit their use. Fortunately this is mainly during the summer months when the majority of Scottish sea angling activity takes place, a season for fish shoals to concentrate on sandeels and herring fry.

Once a minor fishery pursued by small boats was to be found at many Scottish ports, this was the use of the ripper or murderer, a multi hooked lead lure in pursuit of codling. Flies or feathers were also used for mackerel and coalfish, a practice still pursued today by creel fishermen in search of bait.

Feathers, crudely dressed flies, are the original artificial lure used by sea anglers. Even today these should not be spurned as the mobility of a soft feather on a shiny hook gives, underwater, an impression of life and movement.

Tackle shops today stock a wide range of lures for the sea angler, traditional flies may be either dressed with feathers or glittering synthetic materials. To the list can be added plastic squids, now universally known as muppets, rubber eels ranging from simple affairs of rubber tubing to moulded exact replicas of the real thing.

Solid lures armed with single or treble hooks, homemade or bought, can replace sinkers adding an extra hooking chance to the ensemble. When quarry fish shoal to harry smaller fish artificial lures come into their own with heavy bags expected. Fishing can be rapid as no time is wasted baiting hooks with perhaps two or three prime fish hitting the lures as they drop towards the bottom.

Artificial lures must be jigged, moved up and down to impart motion giving the impression of life to inert materials. Quite a useful ploy is to bait feathers or muppets giving the hooks a dual function of both movement and bait scent to attract fish. Remember that there are occasions when artificial baits are totally ineffective with fish only interested in a hook offering which is natural and twitching fresh.

When on the feed, ling can be voracious and two at a time are common

LING - THE OBLIGING FISH

by J. McLanaghan

"She's coming up" yelled the skipper as he scanned the chart on the echo sounder and lines were hastily wound in a few cautious metres. Down below, the sea bed had changed dramatically with the drift. The fairly clean gravel had given way to an upward sweeping jumble of rocks and ledges, a feature which was being reproduced on the graph. Baits for this drift were large fillets of mackerel to a sharp 6/0 hook presented in a style which would impart as much movement as possible. The terminal tackles varied, some had three hooks, some (the more experienced) only one but all were basically paternoster style outfits to keep the hooks clear of any potential snags.

Bounding the baits up the side of the underwater plateau was no job for the lazy or unwary. Anyone who did not keep a tight line lost tackle. The first indication of fish was the pluck on the bait which just dipped the rod tip. This was followed a few seconds later by a more definite unhurried pull as the fish decided to head for home with the bait.

"Ling on" cried the angler and proceeded to work the fish up through the depths, a job which became easier as the fish approached the surface. By the time it came into view the ling was no longer struggling and when it broke surface it was obvious why. It's swim bladder had bloated and was protruding from its mouth. In some fish this is no serious handicap and they can be returned without too much discomfort. The ling, however, is not so forgiving in this respect and should be dispatched immediately. The fish was neatly gaffed, brought on board and put under cover to ensure it was kept in top condition.

This is a fairly typical description of the type of day that anglers in Scotland tend to experience since most ling fishing is done over very rough grounds indeed, as opposed to our southern compatriots whose main catches are from wrecks. Tackle losses can be enormous and it is common place to lose upwards of 10 sets of end gear which can amount to a tidy penny, especially if sinkers are purchased as opposed to home made at a fraction of the price. Indeed, for dirty ground fishing I have seen nuts and bolts and spark plugs all pressed into service.

The ling, like a lot of fish I suppose, can be very easy and very hard to catch at times - a contradiction in terms but let me explain. Having my own boat and small echo sounder, I can potter around for many hours sometimes to locate a mark which I have seen on a chart. I managed at last to find a small upthrust such as I have described and proceeded to fish it under all types of conditions - and take ling. This spot on a good day with a slight breeze could throw up at least one ling per drift (per rod) and the occasional conger eel. Experimentation with end tackle had produced a deadly ling outfit and as a bonus it was fairly snag free. Having proved to myself during a local competition that my gear could produce more fish over a given period than my contemporaries, I decided to go for a biggy on a nearby wreck! The day dawned flat calm, sunny and ideal for the five mile run up the coast. Being a fairly small wreck, it was not too bad to locate but difficult to drift so anchoring was elected to be our mode of attack. Six hours we sat right on top of the wreck hauling up a succession of pollack and coalies but no ling. This wreck, although heavily fished, does not produce any ling of any quantity or quality and on subsequent outings even though I used proven gear I failed to take a single ling.

Movement plays a great part in successful angling and I believe this to be one of the main reasons for an otherwise inexplicable problem. The fact that in one instance I was drifting produced a moving attractive bait covering more terrain and logically more fish. The bait at anchor was doing little other than by scent to attract a fish (although I did vary the height from the wreck). One factor which I have found to be of the highest importance in successful ling angling, or for that matter successful sea angling, is the additional use of an attractor. These can take many and various forms and in the Shetlands where ling are a much sought after species great effort is taken in the making and presentation of baits and attractors. Some of these admittedly are grotesque and cumbersome but they catch fish, further proof if any is needed. My favourite attractor is most simple and consists of a plastic tablespoon with the handle removed, a hole burned through with a nail and a split ring to attach it to the rig. This spoon located within 12" of the hook can be absolutely devastating and is a must also for congers. I have seen it work to great effect (when others go fishless) so I am totally convinced of its efficiency.

The waters around Scotland are top ling areas with plenty of rocky, kelpy terrain but even so it was something of a surprise when the British record toppled to an angler at Stonehaven - a known wreck area but mainly renowned for its big cod. Since the new ling record totally eclipsed the old record it leaves one speculating as to whether this was a pure freak fish or whether it just required the right man with the right gear. There are more than enough records around - commercial records - of big ling to make it fairly certain that the British ling record is far from being safe at almost 58 lbs.

Around the Shetland Islands big ling are no rarity and although not landed every day, a 40 lb. fish raises no eyebrows! Earlier on in the century two fish were brought into Lerwick and they totalled 130 lbs., so an even split makes each a 65 lb. whopper. Commercial fishermen can be-come so blase about big fish but an angling colleague who once worked a boat out of Shetland weighed one very noteworthy fish at over 70 lbs. so the potential is still there. Tackle need not be heavy, since once on the up, ling do not scrap very well and a 30 lb. outfit is ideal for sport and efficiency. I prefer to use a single hook snood of 100 lbs. nylon since the ling have a nice set of molars, my attractor and a 6/0 O'Shaugh-nessy hook complete the bottom end. As a bonus, ling are one of the tastiest fish that can grace a table, with its rich creamy flesh it is a delight.

With the North Sea coming into its own now as a wrecking venue a lot of records could tumble and as interest grows the ling must be a very shaky record. The fish are there, of that I have no doubt, and of all big species available on the wreck scene or on pinnacles, the ling is certainly one of the most obliging.

GUARDING THE RESOURCE

by W.B. Currie

Fishing on the Tay.

In the last eighteen months I have been able to travel and fish in Alaska and travel, but not fish in California. In each case I was impressed by the vastness of the natural resources of the territory. In these vast lands, however, I kept thinking about Scotland, a postage-stamp sized country compared with these huge American states. The collossal fishing resources of Alaska,

which I enjoyed greatly, and the vast mountains and plains of California kept reminding me that we have in Scotland a marvellous, varied landscape, a rich array of fishing waters apd a stock of trout, sea trout and salmon which are exciting to catch and which take us to the depths of the most marvellous country - pocket-sized compared with many regions, but it is, in my mind a pocket full of diamonds.

In Scotland you can travel an hour by car from a Highland centre such as Inverness or Fort William, or others, and reach major and minor salmon rivers, large and small stillwaters and you can, as it is were, sample the whole array of Scottish game fishing. The range is there, in a very small area where there are family fishings in moorland lochs where trout are part of the fun of the day, or beats on salmon rivers where sport can stand with the best salmon fishing in the northern hemisphere.

To guard this resource, and the very special environment of mountain and moor and loch which surrounds it, we have taken many steps to ensure that the quality and purity of the whole landscape is maintained. Scotland has an excellent record in fighting pollution in its rivers, and keeping our environment pure. I can speak with authority on that since I am Chairman of the ACA in Scotland, the body which is dedicated to fighting pollution on behalf of anglers. We have excellent local management and care of our fishings, operated through the newly re-formed district salmon fishery boards, through the excellent work of voluntary bodies such as the Salmon and Trout Association and the Atlantic Salmon

Dee salmon.

Trust. Above all, in recent years we have all benefited from the tremendous initiatives of the Salmon Conservation Trust (Scotland) which has bought out coastal and river netting stations in many parts of Scotland and has ensured easier access of migratory fish into our rivers. But to these is added the excellent work of local angling clubs, many of whom set high standards in cherishing and managing the fishings they control. Individuals, local hotels and local authorities also help. In short (and I have missed out many worthy names) in our small country we have a large proportion of our fishers dedicated to cherishing the waters we love. This is why we have game fishing and a landscape to be proud of and to recommend in Scotland for Fishing. In the countries I have been lucky enough to travel and fish in, while there are individual things we can learn - new techniques of management for example - I have not come across a country as rich in resources and as well conserved and loved as Scotland.

We have, of course, made bad mistakes in the past and may still be making some. The way we have turned over hill land to state and private pulp forestry has caused difficulties for numerous rivers and lochs, both in the management of floods and in water chemistry. We have, in the past, allowed heavy industry and hydro electricity to damage formerly productive rivers. Some of these mistakes have been rectified, including re-establishing at least one major Lowland river (the Clyde) as a salmon water. In some cases, we have been too hasty in overstocking natural lochs with rainbow trout, where a better policy might

have been development of our own wild brown trout fishery. We are not whiter than white, but the interesting thing about Scotland is that, from the grass roots angler up, there is a will to keep the environment in good shape, and to set up the conditions where the land and the fishings can be enjoyed.

In a sense, all of us are fishing travellers. It is not only the visitors to Scotland who drive, explore and fish. Almost every fishing trip I make, for example, involves travel, accommodation, food, fuel and above all, paying for fishing. Scotland is a most natural and rural country, but it must be recognised that its fishings have not only a value, but a cost. It is true that you might find your Highland hotel offering loch trout fishing without charge to guests; it is also true that in certain places, hill loch fishing, burn and hill waters and estuaries might not involve payment, although permission and access must be arranged. Usually our trout fishing costs are very low, often ludicrously low. On the beats of salmon and sea trout rivers, costs reflect the standard of sport and the standard of management which supports the fishing. Again, it is often good value for money. Part of the prices we pay for our fishing underpins the development and care of the fishery and the conservation of our precious environment. But the real force ensuring that Scotland is a marvellous fishing country in world terms is that those who live here and fish here love it and are willing to put their enthusiasm and skills into the task of preserving it and developing it.

River Tweed — a fresh 8lb November fish.

BAIT FOR BIGGIES
by J. McLanaghan

A fine tope taken off the Mull of Galloway — an ideal subject for live baiting.

It's been said before but I'll say it again - fishing's a funny old game. There I was, at my favourite venue Port Logan on the Mull of Galloway, in mid-October doing some tope angling with a few friends. The large mackerel fillet baits were certainly very attractive but the only snag was that they attracted everything but tope. The fishing was literally non-stop with a succession of LSD's, huss, conger and codling, most running to double figures but still not what we wanted.

During a lull at the top of the tide I was having a few moments rest and a well earned cup of tea when I started to contemplate the day's fishing so far. There were plenty of other species showing but no tope. Were there none around? I doubted that. The more likely answer was that the bait wasn't being given time to attract tope before a cod or such gobbled it up. We would soon find out once the ebb started since this venue fishes as well if not better on big ebb tides. True to form, we started to amass a nice box or two of fish - keeping only the cod and occasional conger. A couple of tope runs resulted in one missed and one lost when the hook pulled clear, so there were tope around and prepared to feed if they could get to the bait. Late afternoon saw us boating a

steady stream of codling which now varied from 4 - 7 lbs. all of which fell to large baits meant for tope! On one occasion I had a spirited codling of around 4 lbs on, when my rod gave a sudden dip and line was ripped off my reel. My heart missed a beat as I recalled that Maurice Ashbridge, former European Fish Recorder, had had a similar experience here once before and was left with the head only - and that cod was estimated at over 10 lbs. in weight. Could this be a repeat, a porbeagle? But no, the fish started to come up and I started to wonder if I had imagined it all. That thought was dispelled as the cod broke surface, because hanging grimly on to it was a tope of around 20 -25 lbs.

Totally ignoring the boat and anglers, the tope thrashed around on the surface, his whole being intent on the cod which, was too large a mouthful and, although we lowered fresh mackerel baits alongside him, he ignored these too, eventually swimming off. One week later at exactly the same mark my son had a similar experience but this time the tope was around 45 lbs. and gave the cod a good going over. Once again it ignored baits presented to it. In both cases the fish had totally ignored nicely presented mackerel

A nice catch of cod. These can often attract much more hungry predators.

Even off the shore, live baiting techniques can pay off handsomly.

fillets which were dropped right at their noses in an attempt to take the fish.

Many films have been made regarding the "frenzy" feeding of sharks and their complete dedication to one subject - their prey. This is an aspect of fish behaviour which, although widely known, is not so often utilised in sea angling terms. Live baits are fairly common for some freshwater species but the signals a hooked fish can emit are equally attractive to their saltwater counterparts. Not only are the more obvious predators such as shark and tope the ideal subject for livebaiting but many other species could be profitably fished for in this manner.

For the run of the mill angler the run of the mill baits will suffice but for the specimen hunter looking for a fish better than average he must use a bigger/better bait. Huge pirks have proved their worth at producing big cod, pollack, etc. even a 176 lbs. porbeagle. Not so amazing when you consider the resemblance of a pirk to a wounded fish jerking and jumping in the water. A livebait has several advantages over even a vigorously worked pirk. It looks the real thing, it sounds the real thing, it even tastes the real thing - because it is. The latter point may be a deciding factor on days when big fish are finnicky

and slow to react. Another advantage of the real fish - it is a lot easier to use, no heavy jigging up and down, no expensive losses on bad bottoms and they are plentiful.

Ling is another species of fish which can be added to the livebaiting list and is indeed an avid taker on such tackle. In an area such as a reef or wreck, livebaiting has little useful purpose since the fish population can be taken on almost any lure - so fierce is the competition for food. On open ground or on days when sport is slow, these are the times to use live fish in the hope of an outsize specimen or to get some sort of action started.

There are those who would condemn livebaiting and I can appreciate their views although I may not agree with them. I do not use livebaits very often but I am dedicated enough on occasion to do so when I am prepared to accept a blank day - or a large fish. Like any other bait, it should be used judiciously and can even be used in conjunction with other baits - as I proved on one occasion with great success.

I was fishing a shark festival in Ireland and not a fish had been boated all day in spite of a huge rubby dubby. I was using a full fresh mackerel when a small whiting was brought into the boat. I wound in, added the whiting below the mackerel as a livebait and lowered them into the water. The bait was still decending when it was taken by a blue shark which was promptly boated. Repeating the process, I had two sharks out of four boated within twenty minutes, a clear sign of the taking power of a livebait. Using a livebait which is nicked through at the dorsal fin can ensure the bait remains active for a long while and I make a point of freeing any fish at the end of a session provided it appears fairly vigorous.

Opinions are very divided on the moral nature of livebaiting and it is one arena into which I have no desire to step (or have I already?). What I would advocate is that anglers have an open mind on the subject, a subject that can mean the difference between a blank day and the fish of a lifetime.

A catch of cod off Crail.

SCOTTISH FEDERATION OF SEA ANGLERS

OFFICIALS

President/Chairman
Duncan Mackay
Flat 11b Kirkmichael Road,
Helensburgh

Vice-Presidents
David Neil,
30 Woodfield Road, Ayr

Mrs. Libby Walker
Springvale Cottage, Halket Road
Lugton, by Dunlop, Ayrshire

Hon. Treasurer
Robert Keltie,
76 Stewart Avenue, Bo'ness, West Lothian
EH51 9NW. Tel: (0506) 826274

Secretary/Administrator
Mrs. Helen C. Murray,
Caledonia House, South Gyle,
Edinburgh, EH12 9DQ. Tel: 031-317 7192.

Hon. Fish Recorder
Gordon T. Morris,
8 Burt Avenue, Kinghorn, Fife.
Tel: (0592) 890055

REGIONAL SECRETARIES.

Clyde
A.P. Brown, 32 Swisscot Walk, Fairhill,
Hamilton, ML3 8DX. Tel: (0698) 427085.

Central
Mrs. Margaret McCallum,
58 Pottery Street, Kirkcaldy
KY1 3EU. Tel: (0592) 51710.

West
I.B. McClymont,
41 Corrie Crescent, Saltcoats, Ayrshire

North East
Norman Pickard, 39 Easter Road,
Southside, Kinloss, Forres

Eastern
Mrs. Jeanne Lambert, 47 Gyle Park
Gardens, Edinburgh

Highlands & Islands
David Proudfoot, 3 Bardnaclaven Place,
Janetstown, Thurso, Caithness

Western Isles
F.G. Jefferson, No. 1 Sheshader Point,
Isle of Lewis.

MINIMUM QUALIFYING SIZES OF FISH PRESENTED FOR WEIGH-IN FROM 1 JANUARY 1990.

1.

Bass (Dicentrarchus labrax)	36 cm.	(14.2 in.)
Brill (Scophthalmus rhombus)	30 cm.	(11.8 in.)
Coalfish (Pollachius virens)	35 cm.	(13.8 in.)
Cod (Gadus morhua)	35 cm.	(13.8 in.)
n.b. In U.K. Fishery area V11a from 1st October to		
31 December the minimum size for Cod will be	45 cm.	(17.7 in.)
Dab (Limanda limanda)	23 cm.	(9.06 in.)
Dogfish - all species (Scyliorhinus, Squalius sp)	35 cm.	(13.8 in.)
Eel Common (Anguilla anguilla)	35 cm.	(13.8 in.) ✱✱
Eel Conger (Conger conger)	58 cm.	(22.8 in.)
Flounder (Platichthys flesus)	25 cm.	(9.8 in.)
Haddock (Melanogrammus aeglefinus)	30 cm.	(11.8 in.)
Hake (Merluccius merluccius)	30 cm.	(11.8 in.)
Halibut (Hippoglossus hippoglossus)	35 cm.	(13.8 in.)
Ling (Molva molva)	58 cm.	(22.8 in.) ✱✱
Megrim (Lepidorhombus wiffiagonis)	25 cm.	(9.8 in.)
Pollack (Pollachius pollachius)	35 cm.	(13.8 in.)
Plaice (Pleuronectes platessa)	27 cm.	(10.6 in.)
Rays (Raja sp)	35 cm.	(13.8 in.)
Seabream, Red (Pagellus bogaraveo)	25 cm.	(9.8 in.)
Seabream, Black (Spondyliosoma cantharus)	23 cm.	(9.05 in.)
Shad Twaite (Alosa Fallax)	30 cm.	(11.8 in.)
Skates (Raja batis, alba, oxyrinchus sp)	11.35 kg.	(25 lbs.)
Sole Lemon (Microstomus kitt)	25 cm.	(9.8 in.)
Sole (Solea solea)	24 cm.	(9.4 in.)
Tope (Galeorhinus galeus)	9.10 kg.	(20 lbs.)
Turbot (Scophthalmus maximus)	30 cm.	(11.8 in.)
Whiting (Merlangius merlangus)	27 cm.	(10.6 in.)
Witches (Glyptocephalus gynoglossus)	28 cm.	(11.0 in.)
All other species	20 cm.	(7.9 in.)

✱✱   These sizes may be altered when the European Community determine the new limit for the species.

2. A maximum of three mackerel may be presented for weigh-in.

3. TOPE AND SKATE: Common (R. batis); long-nosed (R. oxyrhinchus) or white (R. alba) are notto be brought ashore during events designated as TOPE or SKATE competitions. They are to be weighed immediately after capture and returned to the sea. (This rule does not apply to potential national record fish which must be brought ashore for weighing.) In designated TOPE competitions no minimum size for weighing will be applied as long as fish are weighed on board and returned alive.

4. Any obviously undersized fish presented for the weigh-in will result in the entrant being disqualified.

SCOTTISH BOAT AND SHORE (rod and line caught)
MARINE FISH RECORDS

B - Boat Records   S - Shore Records   Spec. - Specimen Qualifying Weight

Species		lb.	oz.	dm.	kg.	Place of Capture	Angler	Year	Spec. lb.
ANGLERFISH	B	45	0	0	20.412	Sound of Mull	D. Hopper	1978	20
Lophius piscatorius	S	38	0	0	17.237	Blairmore Pier Loch Long	L. C. Hanley	1970	15
ARGENTINE	B		5	3	0.147	Arrochar	I. Millar	1978	4oz.
Argentina sphyraena	S	OPEN AT ANY WEIGHT							
BARRACUDINA	B	OPEN AT ANY WEIGHT							any
(Paralepis coreganoides									
borealis)	S	0	1	14	0.054	Newton Shore	D. Gillop	1987	1¹/₂oz
BASS	B	8	14	3	4.025	Balcary Bay	D. Shaw	1975	6
Dicentrarchus labrax	S	13	4	0	6.010	Almorness Point	G. Stewart	1975	6
BLACKFISH	B	3	10	8	1.658	Heads of Ayr	J. Semple	1972	2¹/₂
Centrolophus niger	S	OPEN AT ANY WEIGHT							any
BLENNY, SHANNY	B	OPEN AT ANY WEIGHT							any
Blennius pholis	S	0	1	10	0.046	Carolina Port Dundee Docks	M. S. Ettle	1983	1oz.
BLENNY, TOMPOT	B	OPEN AT ANY WEIGHT							any
Blennius gattorugine	S		2	12	0.078	Portpatrick	G. Dods	1977	2oz.
BLENNY VIVIPAROUS	B		10	0	0.283	Craigendoran	T. Lambert	1977	7oz.
Zoarces viviparus	S		11	3	0.317	Craigendoran	D. Ramsay	1975	7oz.
BLENNY, YARREL'S	B	OPEN AT ANY WEIGHT							any
Chirolophis ascanii	S		2	1	0.059	Gourock	D. McEntee	1979	1¹/₂oz.
BLUEMOUTH	B	3	2	8	1.431	Loch Shell	Mrs. A. Lyngholm	1976	2¹/₂
Helicolenus dactylopterus	S	OPEN AT ANY WEIGHT							any
BREAM, BLACK	B	2	9	0	1.162	Kebock Head Lewis	T. Lumb	1974	1
Spondyllosoma cantharus	S	1	13	8	0.836	Gareloch	A. L. Harris	1973	1
BREAM, GILTHEAD	B	OPEN AT ANY WEIGHT							any
Sparus aurata	S	1	1	5	0.490	Dunnet Head	W. Thornton	1988	1
BREAM, RAYS	B	6	3	13	2.829	West of Barra Head	J. Holland	1978	4
Brama brama	S	6	6	8	2.905	Portobello	G. Taylor	1973	4
BREAM RED	B	4	10	0	2.097	Ardnamurchan	R. Steel	1969	1
Pagellus bogaraveo	S	OPEN AT ANY WEIGHT							any
BRILL	B	1	4	0	0.567	Portpatrick	J. Dickson	1984	1
Scophthalmus rhombus	S	1	2	0	0.510	Killintrinnan Lighthouse	P. Baisbrown	1971	1
BULL HUSS	B	20	3	8	9.171	Mull of Galloway	J. K. Crawford	1971	15
Scyliorhinus stellaris	S	15	8	0	7.031	West Tarbet Mull of Galloway	A. K. Paterson	1976	10
BUTTERFISH	B	OPEN AT ANY WEIGHT							any
Pholis gunnellus	S		1	2	0.032	Gourock	D. McEntee	1978	1oz
CATFISH, COMMON	B	13	12	11	6.256	Burnmouth	D. Brown	1985	7
Anachichas lumpus	S	12	12	8	5.797	Stonehaven	G. M. Taylor	1978	4
COALFISH	B	28	4	0	12.814	Eyemouth	L. Gibson	1982	12
Pollachius virens	S	11	7	8	5.202	Loch Long	S. Mather	1976	7
COD	B	46	0	8	20.879	Gantocks	B. Baird	1970	25
Gadus morhua	S	40	11	8	18.470	Balcary Point	K. Robinson	1988	15
DAB	B	2	12	4	1.254	Gairloch	R. Islip	1975	1¹/₂
limanda limanda	S	2	5	0	1.049	Cairnryan	A. Scott	1969	1¹/₂

B - Boat Record   S - Shore record   Spec. - Specimen Qualifying Weight

Species		lb.	oz.	dm.	kg.	Place of Capture	Angler	Year	Spec. lb.
DAB LONG ROUGH	B		6	6	0.180	Helensburgh	J. Napier	1984	4oz
Hippoglossoides platessoides	S		5	8	0.155	Coulport	I. McGrath	1975	4oz
DOGFISH, BLACK-MOUTHED	B	2	13	8	1.288	Loch Fyne	J. H. Anderson	1977	1½
Galeus melastromus	S OPEN AT ANY WEIGHT								any
DOGFISH LESSER-SPOTTED	B	3	15	12	1.807	Portpatrick	R. I. Carruthers	1987	3
Scyliorhinus caniculus	S	4	15	3	2.246	Abbey Burnfoot	S. Ramsay	1988	3
DRAGONET COMMON	B		5	0	0.142	Gareloch	T. J. Ashwell	1985	4oz.
Callionymus lyra	S		5	0	0.143	Loch Long	J. Crawford	1985	4½
EEL, COMMON	B	1	13	7	0.834	Gareloch	P. Fleming	1976	1½
Anguilla anguilla	S	3	0	0	1.360	Ayr Harbour	R. W. Morrice	1972	2
EEL, CONGER	B	48	1		21.820	Largs	R. Bond	1985	30
Conger conger	S	45	0	0	20.411	Scrabster Pier	P. G. Bell	1966	25
FLOUNDER	B	2	13	11	1.295	Portnockie	K. F. Mackay	1985	2½
Platichthys flesus	S	4	11	8	2.140	Musselburgh	R. Armstrong	1970	2½
GARFISH	B	1	11	8	0.799	Brodick	R. Stockwin	1970	1
Belone belone	S	1	11	0	0.764	Bute	Miss McAlorum	1971	1
GOBY BLACK	B		1	4	0.035	Cairnryan	J. Price	1976	1oz
Gobius niger	S		2	4	0.063	Inveraray	F O'Brien	1980	1oz
GURNARD, GREY	B	2	7	0	1.105	Caliach Point	D. Swinbanks	1976	1¾
Eutrigla gurnardus	S	1	5	0	0.595	Peterhead	A. Turnbull	1973	1
		1	5	0	0.595	Port William	J. W. Martin	1977	1
GURNARD, RED	B	2	8	8	1.148	Tobermory	D. V. Relton	1985	1½
Aspitrigla cuculus	S	1	2	5	0.519	Gareloch	G. Smith	1981	12oz.
GURNARD STREAKED	B		10	10	0.301	Isle of Mull	J. Duncan	1985	any
Trigloporus lastoviza	S	1	6	8	0.637	Loch Goil	H. L. Smith	1971	1
GURNARD, TUB	B	5	5	0	2.409	Luce Bay	J. S. Dickinson	1975	3½
Trigla lucerna	S	1	1	0	0.481	Carrick Bay	A. E. Maxwell	1978	12oz.
HADDOCK	B	9	14	12	4.501	Summer Isles	M. Lawton	1980	6
Melanogrammus aeglefinus	S	6	12	0	3.061	Loch Goil	G. B. Stevenson	1976	3
HAKE	B	18	5	8	8.321	Shetland	B. Sinclair	1971	10
Merluccius merluccus	S		11	7	0.324	Gourock	S. Moyes	1979	8oz
HALIBUT	B	234	0		106.136	Scrabster	C. Booth	1979	50
Hippoglossus hippoglossus	S OPEN AT ANY WEIGHT								any
HERRING	B	1	2	0	0.510	Loch Long	R. C. Scott	1974	14oz.
Culpea harengus	S		11	11	0.331	Port Logan	R. Smith	1984	10oz.
LING	B	57	8	0	26.082	Stonehaven	I. Duncan	1982	20
Molva molva	S	12	4	0	5.557	Scrabster	A. Allan	1984	6
LUMPSUCKER	B	4	11	4	2.133	Innellan	G. T. Roebuck	1976	3
Cyclopterus lumpus	S	5	12	10	2.626	Cruden Bay	M. Rennie	1987	3
MACKEREL	B	3	12	0	1.701	Ullapool	E. Scobie	1965	2
Scomber scombrus	S	2	5	9	1.063	Wick	W. Richardson	1969	2
MEGRIM	B	3	12	8	1.715	Gareloch	P. Christie	1973	2
Lepidorhombus whiffiagonis	S	1	11	6	0.325	Loch Ryan	C. N. Dickson	1989	any
MULLETT, GOLDEN GREY	B OPEN AT ANY WEIGHT								any
Lisa aurata	S		11	0	0.312	Fairlie	I. McFadyen	1972	8oz.

Species		lb.	oz.	dm.	kg.	Place of Capture	Angler	Year	Spec lb.
MULLET, THICK LIPPED GREY	B	3	6	0	1.531	Luce Bay	R. Williamson	1976	3
Crenimugil labrosus	S	6	7	8	2.934	Ayr Harbour	D.A. Smith	1984	4½
NORWAY HADDOCK	B	1	10	5	0.750	Eyemouth	P. Skala	1988	14oz.
Sebastes viviparus	S	OPEN AT ANY WEIGHT							any
PIPEFISH GREATER	B	OPEN AT ANY WEIGHT							any
Sygnathus acus	S		0	13	0.023	Coulport	H. Holding	1975	any
PLAICE	B	10	3	8	4.635	Longa Sound	H. Gardiner	1974	5
Pleuronectes platessa	S	5	8	0	2.494	Arrochar	A. Holt Jnr.	1971	3½
POLLACK	B	18	0	0	8.165	Scrabster	N. Carter	1971	10
Pollachius pollachius	S	13	14	0	6.293	Furnace	J. Arthur	1974	8
POOR COD	B	1	4	0	0.567	Arbroath	F. Chalmers	1969	1
Trisopterus minutus	S	1	0	0	0.453	Loch Fyne	F. Johnstone	1970	12oz.
POUTING	B	3	8	0	1.587	Gourock	J. Lewis	1977	2
Trisopterus luscus	S	3	3	7	1.458	Kirkcudbright	R. Cartwright	1984	1½
RAY BLONDE	B	26	11	0	12.105	Caliach Point	B. Swinbanks	1977	15
Raja brachyura	S	OPEN AT ANY WEIGHT							any
RAY CUCKOO	B	5	4	4	2.388	Gairloch	A. Bridges	1979	4
Raja naevus	S	4	11	0	2.126	Gourock	R.A.H. McCaw	1973	3¾
RAY SPOTTED	B	8	3	14	3.739	Isle of Whithorn	G. Brownlie	1989	4
Raja montagui	S	5	12	0	2.608	Cairnryan	G C.Styles	1975	4
RAY THORNBACK	B	29	8	10	13.399	Luce bay	A. McLean	1982	15
Raja clavata	S	21	12		9.866	Kirkcudbright	S.Ramsay	1985	4
ROCKLING, FIVE BEARDED	B	OPEN AT ANY WEIGHT							any
Ciliata mustela	S		7	0	0.198	Balcarry Point	K. Greason	1988	4½oz.
ROCKLING, FOUR BEARDED	B		1	7	0.040	Gourock	S. Hodgson	1981	1¼oz.
Rhinomenus cimbrius	S	OPEN AT ANY WEIGHT							any
ROCKLING SHORE	B	OPEN AT ANY WEIGHT							any
Gairdropsarus mediterraneus	S		14	8	0.411	Loch Long	A. Glen	1982	7oz.
ROCKLING, THREE BEARDED	B	1	14	4	0.857	Stonehaven	W. Murphy	1972	1¼
Gairdropsaus vulgaris	S	2	11	9	1.235	Kircudbright	A. Johnstone	1981	1½
SANDEEL, GREATER	B		8	0	0.227	Caliach Point	T.J. Ashwell	1984	6oz.
Hyperoplus lanceolatus	S	0	4	4	0.120	Isle of Lewis	R. McMillan	1987	3oz.
SCAD (HORSE MACKEREL)	B	1	7	0	0.652	Loch Sheil	D. MacNeil	1976	1
Trachurus trachurus	S	3	0	14	1.384	Cockenzie	R. Dillon	1981	1
SEA SCORPION, LONGSPINED	B		3	6	0.096	Rhu Narrows	C. Heath	1985	2½oz.
Taurulus bubalis	S		5	9	0.157	Aberdeen	T.J. Ashwell	1982	2½oz.
SEA SCORPION SHORTSPINED	B	2	3	0	0.992	Kepple Pier	R. Stevenson	1973	1¾
Myoxocephalus scorpius	S	2	3	0	0.992	Cloch, Gourock	W. Crawford	1979	1½
SHAD, TWAITE	B	OPEN AT ANY WEIGHT							any
Alosa fallax	S	2	12	0	1.247	Garlieston	J.W. Martin	1978	1½
SHARK, BLUE	B	85	8	0	38.781	Stornoway	J. Morrison	1972	50
Prionace glauca	S	OPEN AT ANY WEIGHT							any

Species	lb.	oz.	dm.	kg.	Place of Capture	Angler	Year	Spec. lb.
SHARK PORBEAGLE	B 404	0	0	183.244	Sumburgh Head	P. White	1976	300
Lamna nasus	B 404	0	0	183.244	Sumburgh Head	P. White	1978	300
	S OPEN AT ANY WEIGHT							any
SKATE, COMMON	B 227	0	0	102.967	Tobermory	R. Banks	1986	100
Raja batis	S 154	0	0	69.854	Achiltibuie	M.J. Traynor	1971	50
SMELT	B OPEN AT ANY WEIGHT							any
Osmerus Eperlanus	S	5	4	0.149	Riverside, Dundee	M. Ettle	1988	4¹/2oz.
SMOOTHHOUND	B OPEN AT ANY WEIGHT							any
STARRY								
Mustelus asterias	S	7	12	14 3.540	Kirkcudbright	M. Roberts	1987	5
SOLE, DOVER	B	1	12	0 0.793	Killintrinnon	W. Hannah	1974	1
Solea Solea	S	2	0	8 0.922	Balcary	W. Lees	1989	8oz
SOLE LEMON	B	2	2	0 0.963	Lochgoilhead	J. Gordon	1976	1
Microstomus kitt	S	1	6	2 0.627	Peterhead	B N. Davidson	1982	12oz.
SPURDOG	B	18	14	0 8.560	Tobermory	J. Bean	1988	14
Squalus acanthias	S	12	8	12 5.691	Millport	R. Paterson	1983	8
TADPOLE FISH	B		14	14 0.421	Firth of Clyde	R. Donnelly	1981	8oz
Raniceps raninus	S	1	3	0 0.538	Dunbar	W. Dickson	1977	10oz.
TOPE	B	74	11	0 33.877	Loch Ryan	P. Marsland	1989	45
Galeorhinus galeus	S	54	4	0 24.606	Loch Ryan	D. Hastings	1975	30
TOPKNOT	B OPEN AT ANY WEIGHT							any
Zeugopterus	S		8	8 0.241	Peterhead	G.M. Taylor	1975	6oz.
punctatus								
TORSK	B	15	7	2 7.006	Pentland Firth	D.J. Mackay	1982	8
Brosme brosme	S OPEN AT ANY WEIGHT							any
TURBOT	B	25	4	0 11.453	Mull	I. Jenkins	1982	15
Scophthalmus	S	2	13	12 1.300	Cairnryan	G. Calderwood	1989	1
maximus								
WEAVER GREATER	B OPEN AT ANY WEIGHT							any
Trachinus draco	S	1	1	14 0.508	Mull of Galloway	W. Allison	1984	1
WHITING	B	6	8	0 2.948	Girvan	A M Devay	1969	3
Merlangius merlangus	S	3	0	0 1.360	Gourock	D. McTehee	1970	2
WHITING BLUE	B	1	12	0 0.793	Loch Fyne	J.H. Anderson	1977	8oz.
(POUTASSOU)								
Micromesistius	S OPEN AT ANY WEIGHT							any
poutassou								
WRASSE BALLAN	B	4	12	4 2.161	Calgary Bay, Mull	K F.J. Hall	1983	3¹/2
Labrus bergylta	S	5	0	0 2.268	Girvan	T. McGeehan	1971	3¹/2
WRASSE CORKWING	B OPEN AT ANY WEIGHT							any
Crenilabrus melops	S		6	3 0.175	Wigton Pen.	I. Wilson	1989	4oz
WRASSE CUCKOO	B	3	0	0 1.361	Scrabster	Mrs. H. Campbell	1969	1¹/4
Labrus mixtus	S	1	2	0 0.510	Neist Point, Skye	Q.A. Oliver	1972	12oz.
WRASSE	B	0	0	12 0.021	Lochaline	D. D. Morrison	1983	1oz.
GOLDSINNY								
Ctenolabrus rupestris	S		1	13 0.051	Loch Goil	T. Lambert	1977	1¹/2oz.
			1	13 0.051	Mull of Galloway	G.V.R. Griffiths	1985	1¹/2oz.
WRASSE	B OPEN AT ANY WEIGHT							any
SMALL MOUTHED								
ROCK COOK								
Centrolabrus exoletus	S		2	0 0.056	Achiltibuie Pier	D.F. McKendrick	1985	1¹/2oz.
WRASSE, SCALE	B	0	10	15 0.310	Tobermory	J. Teal	1986	8oz.
RAYED								
Acantholabrus palloni	S OPEN AT ANY WEIGHT							any

The above records are based on information received up to 30th September, 1989, by the S.F.S.A. Honorary Fish Recorder, G. T. Morris, 8 Burt Avenue, Kinghorn, Fife.

A N G U S

ARGYLLSHIRE AYRSHIRE BANFFSHIRE CAITHNESS

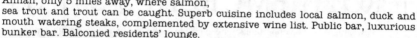

DUMFRIESSHIRE

FIFE

BANCHORY LODGE HOTEL

TEL: (033 02) 2625
Banchory AB3 3HS

Hosts: Mr. & Mrs. D.B. Jaffray
25 bedrooms. Closed January.
Picturesque and tranquil setting
overlooking River Dee.
*Country house with private fishing
and luxurious accommodation.*

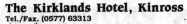

KINCARDINESHIRE

KINROSS

KIRKCUDBRIGHT

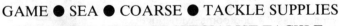

PLEASE SEE PAGES 139-144 FOR ROAD MAPS

70

P E R T H S H I R E

R O S S - S H I R E

76

Manderston

BORDERS

Area Tourist Board
Scottish Borders Tourist Board

Director of Tourism
Scottish Borders Tourist Board
Municipal Buildings
High Street
Selkirk TD7 4JX.
Tel: Selkirk (0750) 20555

RIVER PURIFICATION BOARD
TWEED RIVER PURIFICATION BOARD
Burnbrae
Mossilee Road
Galashiels.
Tel: Galashiels 2425

RIVERS

Water	Location	Species	Season	Permit available from	Other Information
Blackadder	Greenlaw	Brown Trout	1 Apr. to 6 Oct.	Greenlaw Angling Club J. Purves, 9 Wester Row, Greenlaw.	No bait fishing till 15 Apr. Sunday fishing. No spinning. No Sunday competitions.
Eden Water	Kelso	Brown Trout	1 Apr. to 30 Sept.	Forrest & Sons, 35 The Square, Kelso. Tel: 24687. Intersport, 43 The Square, Kelso. Springwood Caravan Park, Kelso TD5 8LS. Tel: (0573) 24596. Border Hotel, Woodmarket, Kelso TD5 7AX. Tel: 0573 24791.	Fly only. No spinning. Restricted to 3 rods.
	Gordon	Brown Trout	15 Mar. to 6 Oct.	J.H. Fairgrieve, Burnbrae, Gordon. Tel: 357.	No Spinning. No Sunday fishing.
Ettrick & Yarrow	Bowhill	Salmon Trout	1 Feb.-30 Nov. 15 Mar.-30 Sep.	Buccleuch Estates, Bowhill, Selkirk. Tel: (0750) 20753.	
	Selkirk	Brown Trout	1 Apr. to 30 Sept.	Selkirk & District Angling Association. A. Murray, 40 Raeburn Meadow, Selkirk.	Night fishing 15 May-14 Sept. Week ticket only. No minnows or spinning. No Sundays.
Ettrick	Ettrick Bridge	Brown Trout Salmon	1 Apr.-30 Sep. 1 Feb.-30 Nov.	Ettrickshaws Hotel, Tel: (0750) 52229.	Packed Lunches and flask for residents. Permits also available for other waters.
Kale Water	Eckford	Trout Grayling	1 Apr. to 30 Sept.	Gamekeeper, No. 4 Eckford. Mr. Graham, Eckford Cottage, Eckford, Kelso. Tel: (083-55) 255.	No Sundays.
	Morebattle	Trout Grayling	15 Mar. to 6 Oct.	D.Y. Gray, 17 Mainsfield Avenue, Morebattle. The Garage, Morebattle. Templehall Hotel, Morebattle.	No ground baiting. No Sunday fishing.

Water	Location	Species	Season	Permit available from	Other Information
Leader Water	Lauderdale	Trout	15 Mar. to 6 Oct.	Lauderdale Angling Association, D.M. Milligan, 1 Newbyth House Stables, East Linton. Lauder Post Office. Tower Hotel, Oxton. The Chip Shop. Anglers Choice, 23 Market Square, Melrose TD6 9PL. Tel: (089 682) 3070.	No Spinning. Sunday fishing. No Grayling fishing.
Leader Water/ Tweed	Earlston	Trout	15 Mar. to 30 Sept.	Earlston Angling Association P. Hessett, 2 Arnot Place, Earlston. Tel: 577. E. & M. Browne, Newsagent, Earlston. L. & M. Pollard Newsagents, The Square, Earlston. Anglers Choice, 23 Market Square, Melrose. Tel: (089 682) 3070. Wilson, Saddlers, Dalkeith. Hotels & pubs. Tweed Permits from J. Yule, Cullen Cottage, Eastgreen, Earlston. Tel: 216.	No Sunday fishing. Other restrictions as per permit.
Liddle Water	Newcastleton	Sea Trout	1 May to 30 Sept.	J.D. Ewart, Fishing Tackle Shop, Newcastleton. Tel: (03873) 75257.	
		Brown Trout	15 Apr. to 30 Sept.	Mrs. B. Elliot, Thistlesyke, Newcastleton. Tel: Liddlesdale 75200.	
	South Roxburgh- shire	Salmon Sea Trout Herling Brown Trout	1 Feb.-31 Oct. 1 May to 30 Sept. 15 Apr. to 30 Sept.	Esk & Liddle Fisheries Assoc. per R.J.B. Hill, Sec. Bank of Scotland Buildings, Langholm. Tel: (03873) 80428. George Graham, Hagg-on-Esk, Old School, Canonbie. Tel: (03873) 71416. Peter Lillie, 19 Rowanburn, Canonbie. Tel: (03873) 71224.	Spinning allowed until 14 Apr. and otherwise only when water is above markers at Newcastleton, Kershopefoot and Penton Bridges. No Sunday fishing.
Lyne Water	Tweed Junction to Flemington Bridge	Trout Grayling	1 Apr. to 30 Sept.	Peebleshire Trout Fishing Association D.G. Fyfe, 39 High Street, Peebles. Tel: 20131. I. Fraser, Northgate, Peebles. Tel: 20979. Tweed Valley Hotel, Walkerburn. Tel: (089 687) 636. J. Dickson & Son, 21 Frederick Street, Edinburgh. Tel: 031-225 4218. Crook Inn, Tweedsmuir.	No Sundays. No spinning. No bait fishing April & Sept. Tickets also cover Tweed.

Water	Location	Species	Season	Permit available from	Other Information
Teviot	Kelso	Trout Grayling	1 Apr. to 30 Sept.	Kelso Angling Association Mr. R. Yule, 6 Highcroft, Kelso. Tel: Kelso 23907. Forrest & Sons, 35, The Square, Kelso. Tel: Kelso 24687. Intersport, 43, The Square, Kelso. Border Hotel. Springwood Caravan Park. Kelso TD5 8LS. Tel: (0573) 24596.	No Sundays. Restrictions on spinning. No maggots or ground bait. Size limit 10".
	Eckford	Salmon Sea Trout Brown Trout	1 Feb.-30 Nov. 15 Mar. to 30 Sep.	Gamekeeper, No. 4, Eckford Mr. Graham Eckford Cottage, Eckford, Kelso. Tel: (083-55) 255.	No Sundays. Limited to 4 day permits. Bait and spinning 15 Feb.-15 Sept. only. Spinning for Trout and Grayling prohibited.
	Jedforest	Salmon	1 Feb. to 31 Nov.	Jedforest Angling Association J.T. Renilson, 4 Canongate, Jedburgh.	No Sundays. Salmon: 4 rods per day. Spinning 15 Feb.-14 Sept. Fly only 15 Sept.-30 Nov.
Teviot (and Ale Slitrig Borthwick Rule)	Hawick	Brown Trout	15 Mar. to 30 Sept.	Porteous & Newcombe, Howgate, Hawick.	All rules and regulations on ticket.
		Salmon	1 Feb. to 30 Nov.	The Pet Store, Union Street, Hawick.	
		Grayling	1 Jan. to 30 Sept.	Club Premises, 5 Sandbed, Lindsays Grocers, Denholm.	
Teviot	Above Chesters	Salmon Sea Trout	1 Feb. to 30 Nov.	The Pet Store, Union Street, Hawick.	All rules and regulations on ticket. Limited to 4 rods per day. 6 visitors tickets only on application to: Mr. R.A. Sutherland, Hawick Angling Club, 20 Longhope Drive, Hawick TD9 0DU. Tel: 0450 75150.
Tweed	Tweedsmuir	Brown Trout Grayling	1 Oct. to 30 Nov.	Crook Inn, Tweedsmuir. Tel: (08997) 272.	All rules and regulations on permits.
	Peebleshire (substantial stretch of river)	Trout Grayling	1 Apr. to 30 Sept.	Ian Fraser Sports, 1 Bridgegate, Peebles. Tel: 20979. Tweed Valley Hotel, Walkerburn. Tel: (089 687) 636. F. & D. Simpson, 28 West Preston Street, Edinburgh. Tel: 031-667 3058. J. Dickson & Son, 21 Frederick Street, Edinburgh. Tel: 031-225 4218.	No spinning. No bait fishing, Apr. & Sept. No Sunday fishing. Tickets also cover Lyne Water. Waders desirable. Fly only on Tweed from Lynefoot upstream.

Water	Location	Species	Season	Permit available from	Other Information
Tweed cont.	Peebles (Wire Bridge Pool to Nutwood Pool - excluding Kailzie)	Salmon	21 Feb. to 30 Nov.	Peebleshire Salmon Fishing Association Seasons: Blackwood & Smith, W.S., 39 High Street, Peebles. Tel: 20131. Days: I. Fraser, Northgate, Peebles. Tel: 20979.	Fly fishing only. No Sundays. Other regulations on tickets.
	Peebles	Salmon	21 Feb. to 30 Nov.	Residents: Tweeddale District permit applies.	Restricted to 20 per day. No seasons for visitors. Advance booking advisable Sept. to Nov. No Sundays. No swivels. Other regulations as Peebleshire Salmon Fishing Association.
	Walkerburn	Salmon/ Sea Trout Trout	1 Feb.to 30 Nov. 1 Apr.-30 Sep.	Tweed Valley Hotel, Walkerburn. Tel: (089 687) 636.	Salmon tickets for hotel guests only after 14 Sept. Special salmon and trout weeks, tuition. Trout and grayling permits available to all.
	Peel	Salmon Sea Trout	15 Feb. to 30 Nov.	Tweed Valley Hotel, Walkerburn. Tel: (089 687) 636.	Private 2-rod salmon beat on south bank.
	Nest	Salmon Sea Trout Trout	1 Feb.to 30 Nov. 1 Apr.-20 Sep.	Tweed Valley Hotel, Walkerburn. Tel: (089 687) 636.	Private salmon/sea trout beat approx. 1¼ miles, 4 rods. Fly only 15 Sept. to 30 Nov. Trout and grayling permits available to all.
	Ashiestiel (Nest and Peel)	Salmon Sea Trout Trout	1 Feb. to 30 Nov. 1 Apr. to 30 Sept.	Tweed Valley Hotel, Walkerburn. Tel: (089 687) 636 2½ miles south bank. Week or day lets Spring/Summer. Week lets only October and November. Angling Course September.	
	Haystoun	Salmon	1 Feb. to 30 Nov.	I. Fraser Sports, Northgate, Peebles. Tel: 20979.	Spinning allowed 15 Feb. to 14 Sept. 1½ miles in length. 8 named salmon pools.
	Kingsmeadow	Salmon	1 Feb. to 30 Nov.	I. Fraser Sports, Northgate, Peebles. Tel: 20979.	Spinning allowed. 15 Feb to 14 Sept. ¾ miles in length. 5 named salmon pools.
	Glenormiston	Salmon	1 Feb. to 30 Nov.	I. Fraser Sports, Northgate, Peebles. Tel: 20979.	Fly only. 1 mile in length. 5 named salmon pools.
	Galashiels	Trout	1 Apr. to 30 Sept.	Messrs. J. & A. Turnbull, 30 Bank Street, Galashiels. Tel: 3191. Kingsknowes Hotel, Galashiels. Tel: (0896) 58375.	No Sundays. Day tickets available on Saturdays. No spinning.

Water	Location	Species	Season	Permit available from	Other Information
Tweed contd.	Melrose	Trout Grayling	1 Apr.to 6 Oct. 7 Oct.to 15 Mar.	Melrose & District Angling Association Anglers Choice, 23 Market Square, Melrose. Tel: 3070.	No spinning. No ground baiting. No Sundays. Minnow fishing not permitted. Spinning reels of all types prohibited.
	Melrose (Ravenswood Tweedswood)	Brown Trout	1 Apr. to 30 Sept.	Anglers Choice, 23 Market Square, Melrose. Tel: 3070.	
	Melrose (Pavilion)	Salmon Sea Trout	1 Feb. to 30 Nov.	Anglers Choice, 23 Market Square, Melrose. Tel: 3070.	Fly only - 1 to 15 Feb. and 15 Sept. to 30 Nov. Feb. 16 to Sept. 14 fly and spinning.
	St. Boswells	Brown Trout Trout	1 Apr. to 30 Sept.	St. Boswells Angling Association Mr. Law, Main Street, St. Boswells. Dryburgh Abbey Hotel, St. Boswells. Tel: (0835) 22261. Anglers Choice, 23 Market Square, Melrose. Miss A. Laing, Newsagent, St. Boswells.	Fly only 1 Apr. to 1 May. No ground baiting. No bait fishing until May 1. No Sundays. No spinning tackle. No coarse fishing allowed outside season. Access to restricted beats by special permits only. Full details shown on permit.
Tweed (and Teviot)	Kelso	Trout	1Apr. to 30 Sept.	Kelso Angling Association Mr. R. Yule, 6 High Croft, Kelso. Tel: 23907.	No Sundays. Size limit 10in. Fly only 1-30 April.
		Grayling	1 May-31 Aug. 1 Dec.-31 Jan.	Forrest & Sons, 35, The Square, Kelso. Tel: (0573) 24687. Intersport, 43, The Square, Kelso. Borders Hotel, Woodmarket, Kelso. Tel: (0573) 24791. Springwood Caravan Park.	Spinning restrictions. No maggots or ground bait. No fishing above Roxburgh Viaduct between 15 & 30 Sept. incl.
		Salmon Trout Grayling Brown Trout Coarse		Tweedside Tackle, 32 Woodmarket, Kelso TD5 7AX. Tel: (0573) 25306.	Day/week/season.
Tweed	Kelso	Brown Trout Coarse Fish	1 Apr. to 30 Sept.	Forrest & Sons, 35, The Square, Kelso. Tel: (0573) 24687.	
	Cornhill	Salmon Sea Trout Brown Trout Salmon	1 Feb. to 30 Nov.	Tillmouth Park Hotel, Cornhill-on-Tweed, Northumberland TD12 4UU. Tel: (0890) 2255.	No Sundays. No worming. Boats and ghillies available. Special terms for residents.
	Ladykirk	Brown Trout	19 Mar. to 8 Oct.	Victoria Hotel, Norham, Tel: (0289) 82237.	No spinning. No ground baiting. Fly only above Norham Bridge to West Ford. No Sundays.

Water	Location	Species	Season	Permit available from	Other Information
Tweed contd.	Horncliffe (Tidal)	Trout, Grayling, Roach, Dace and Eel.		No permit required.	
Whiteadder & Dye & Tributaries	30 miles	Brown/ Rainbow Trout	15 Mar. to 30 Sept.	Whiteadder Angling Association Mr. Cowan, Crumstane, Duns. (Bailiff). Tel: (0361) 83235.	No Sundays. Fly only before 15 Apr. Worm from 15 Apr. only. Minnow from 1 May only. Tickets in advance. Size limit 8 inches. River stocked annually.
Whiteadder	Allanton	Trout	2 Apr. to 30 Sept.	Berwick & District Angling Association. Mr. D. Cowan, 3 Church Street, Berwick. Tel: (0289) 330145.	Fly only before May. No spinning. No threadline. No maggot fishing. No ground baiting. 9 inch min. Max bag of 12 brown trout per day. No Sundays.

LOCHS AND RESERVOIRS

Water	Location	Species	Season	Permit available from	Other Information
Acreknowe Reservoir	Hawick	Brown/ Rainbow Trout	15 Mar. to end Sept.	Porteous & Newcome, Howgate, Hawick. The Pet Shop, Union Street, Hawick. Mr. R.A. Sutherland, 20 Longhope Drive, Hawick. Tel: (0450) 75150.	Ticket covers all other trout waters managed by Hawick Angling Club. Boat available from Pet Shop.
Alemoor Loch	Hawick	Brown Trout Perch Pike		As Acreknowe	Bank fishing only.
Hellmoor Loch	Hawick	Brown Trout		As Acreknowe	No Boat. No competitions. Limit 6 trout.
Loch of the Lowes and St. Mary's Loch	Selkirk	Brown Trout	1 Apr. to 30 Sept.	St. Mary's A.C. per Sec. J. Miller, 8/5 Craighouse Gardens, Edinburgh. Tel: 031-447 0024.	Fly fishing only, until 30th April thereafter spinning and bait allowed.
		Pike Perch Eels	1 May to 30 Sept.	Tibbiesheils Hotel (Lochside). Anglers Choice, 23 Market Square, Melrose. Rodono Hotel (Loch side). Sonny's Sports Shop, 29 High Street, Innerleithen.	Club fishing apply in advance to Secretary or keeper. Sunday fishing allowed. Weekly permits are obtainable from the keeper. No float fishing. Boats from keeper only. River Tweed Protection Order applies. Club memberships available.
Peebleshire Lochs	Tweed Valley	Brown/ Rainbow Trout	Apr. to Oct.	Tweed Valley Hotel, Walkerburn. Tel: (089 687) 636.	Stocked private lochans.
Synton Loch	Hawick	Brown Trout		As Acreknowe Reservoir.	Boats available From Pet Store, 1 Union Street, Hawick.

Water	Location	Species	Season	Permit available from	Other Information
Upper Loch	Bowhill	Brown/ Rainbow Trout	1 Apr. to 5 Oct.	Buccleuch Estate, Bowhill, Selkirk. Tel: (0750) 20753.	Fly only. 2 rods per boat and limit of 8 fish per boat.
Watch Reservoir	Longformacus	Brown Trout Rainbow Trout	15 Mar.-30 Sept. All year	W.F. Renton, The Watch Fly Reservoir, Tel: (03617) 331 & (0289) 306028.	Sunday fishing. Fly only. Strictly no use of bait/maggots etc.
Williestruther Loch	Hawick	Brown/ Rainbow Trout	As Acreknowe Reservoir.	Limit of 2 rainbow per day. Limit of 4 brown trout.	
Wooden Loch	Eckford	Brown Trout	1 Apr. to 30 Sept.	Gamekeeper, No. 4 Eckford Mr. Graham	One boat. No bank fishing. Only rainbow trout after
		Rainbow Trout	1 Apr. to 31 Oct.	Eckford Cott. Eckford, Kelso. Tel: (083-55) 255	30 Sept. Only 3 rods at any time. Advance booking necessary. No Sundays.

BORDERS
Sea Angling

The Scottish Borders provide some of the best sea angling in the UK. Based on Eyemouth, which has the largest fishing fleet in the South of Scotland, and the smaller fishing villages of Burnmouth and St. Abbs, the clear unpolluted waters are well stocked with a wide variety of sea fish. So clear is the water that one of the first Marine Reservations has been established off Eyemouth. The rugged coastline with its unique fauna make a spectacular background to your day's fishing.

It should be noted that sea angling is not permitted off St. Abbs Head National Reserve (Petticowick – Long Carr).
Eyemouth is only nine miles north of Berwick-upon-Tweed, just off the A.1. Its colourful boats, fish auction and sandy beach make it a popular resort during the summer. Well known for its excellent rock fishing, the town is also a useful point of access to shoreline to the north and south. Boat fishing has developed over the years due to the efforts of Eyemouth Sea Angling Club who now run a number of shore and boat competitions throughout the season.

The club operates the coast from Burnmouth harbour in the south to the harbour at St. Abbs in the north.

Types of fish: Shore – cod, mackerel, coalfish, flounder, plaice, sole, haddock, whiting, catfish, ling and wrasse.
Boat – the same species can be caught as on shore but larger specimens.

Boats: A large number of fishing boats are usually available from Eyemouth, St. Abbs and Burnmouth for parties of anglers at weekends.

Area Tourist Board
Dumfries and Galloway Tourist Board

Director of Tourism,
Dumfries and Galloway Tourist Board
Douglas House,
Newton Stewart,
Wigtownshire DG8 6DQ.
Tel: Newton Stewart (0671) 2549

RIVER PURIFICATION BOARD
SOLWAY RIVER PURIFICATION BOARD
River's House, Irongray Road,
Dumfries DG2 0JE.
Tel: Dumfries 720502.

RIVERS

Water	Location	Species	Season	Permit available from	Other information
Annan	Hoddom & Kinmount Estates Ecclefechan	Salmon Sea Trout Brown Trout	25 Feb. to 15 Nov.	Miss Marsh, 2 Bridge End Cottage, Hoddom, Lockerbie DG11 1BE. Tel: (05763) 488.	No Sunday fishing. Fly water unless the spinning mark is covered.
	Halleaths Estate Lockerbie	Salmon Sea Trout	25 Feb. to 15 Nov.	Messrs. McJerrow & Stevenson, Solicitors, Lockerbie, Dumfriesshire. Tel: Lockerbie 2123.	Limited number of tickets.
	Royal Four Towns Water Lockerbie	Salmon Sea Trout Brown Trout Herling Chub Grilse	25 Feb. to 15 Nov.	Clerk to the Commissioners, of Royal Four Towns Fishing Mrs. K. Ratcliffe, Clerk, 'Jay-Ar', Preston House Road, Hightae, Lockerbie. Tel: 0387 810220.	Boats prohibited. Fly and spinning. No Sunday fishing.
	St. Mungo Parish	Salmon Sea Trout	25 Feb. to 15 Nov.	Castle Milk Estates Office, Norwood, Lockerbie.	Fly fishing only. No Sunday fishing.
		Brown Trout	15 Mar. to 6 Oct.	Tel: Kettleholm 203/4.	
	Mount Annan Beat	Salmon Sea Trout Brown Trout	25 Feb. to 15 Nov.	Mrs. Brooke, Mount Annan, Annan. Tel: (04612) 2186.	Limited number of tickets. No Sunday fishing. Restrictions depend on water level.
	Warmanbie Estate	Salmon Sea Trout Brown Trout	25 Feb. to 15 Nov.	Warmanbie Hotel & Restaurant, Annan DG12 5LL. Tel: (04612) 4015.	Fly, spinning, worm all season.
	Lockerbie	Salmon Trout Coarse		Dryfesdale Hotel, Lockerbie, Dumfriesshire.	
Bladnoch	Newton Stewart	Salmon	1 Mar. to 30 Sept.	Newton Stewart Angling Association Galloway Guns & Tackle, Arthur Street, Newton Stewart. Tel: (0671) 3404.	
Cairn	Dumfries	Salmon Sea Trout		Dumfries & Galloway Angling Association, Secretary: D. Byers, 4 Bloomfield Edinburgh Road, Dumfries DG1 1SG. Tel: (0387) 53850.	Limited number of permits. No Sunday fishing. Restrictions depend on

Water	Location	Species	Season	Permit available from	Other information
Cairn contd.		Brown Trout	15 Mar. to 31 Aug.		Water level. Visitors Mon.-Fri. only.
Cree (and Pencill Burn)	Drumlamford Estate	Salmon Trout Coarse	April to October	The Keeper, The Kennels, Drumlamford Estate, Barrhill. Tel: (046 582) 220.	
	Newton Stewart	Salmon Sea Trout	1 Mar. to 14 Oct.	Newton Stewart Angling Association Galloway Guns & Tackle, Arthur Street, Newton Stewart. Tel: (0671) 3404.	No Sunday fishing.
Cross Waters of Luce	New Luce	Salmon Sea Trout	1 May to 31 Oct.	Stranraer & District Angling Association. The Sports Shop, 90 George Street, Stranraer. Tel: (0776) 2705. Park House Hotel, Dunragit.	No Sunday fishing. Live lobworm, branderings & magggots; fresh water baits. Day permits available for Piltanton Burn from Dunragit Angling Club.
Dee	Aboyne	Salmon Sea Trout Rainbow Trout	1 Feb. to 30 Sep.	Brooks House, Glen Tanar, Aboyne. Tel: (03398) 86451.	No Sunday fishing on Dee. Fly fishing only.
Black Water of Dee	Mossdale	Salmon	11 Feb. to 31 Oct.	New Galloway Angling Association, Secretary, A. Cairnie, Garsons Knowe, New Galloway.	
		Trout Pike Perch	15 Mar. to 30 Sept.	Local Hotels.	
Esk	East Dumfriesshire	Salmon Sea Trout/ Herling Brown Trout	1 Feb.to 31 Oct. 1 May to 30 Sept. 15 Apr. to 30 Sept.	Esk & Liddle Fisheries Association per R.J.B. Hill, Secretary, Bank of Scotland Buildings, Langholm. Tel: (03873) 80428. George Graham, Hagg-on-Esk, Old School, Canonbie. Tel: (03873) 71416. Peter Lillie, 19 Rowanburn, Canonbie. Tel: (03873) 71224.	Spinning allowed until 14 April and otherwise only when water is above markers at Skippers Bridge, Canonbie Bridge & Willow Pool. No Sunday fishing.
Ewes, Wauchope, Tarras	East Dumfriesshire	Salmon Sea Trout/ Herling Brown Trout	1 Feb.-31 Oct. 1 May to 30 Sept. 15 Apr. to 30 Sept.	Esk & Liddle Fisheries Association per R.J.B. Hill, Secretary, Bank of Scotland Buildings, Langholm. Tel: 03873 80428. George Graham, Hagg-on-Esk, Old School, Canonbie, Dumfriesshire. Tel: 03873 71416.	Spinning allowed only until 14 April. No Sunday fishing.
Liddle	Newcastleton Ticket	Salmon Sea Trout Brown Trout	15 Apr.-31 Oct. 1 May-30 Sept. 15 Apr.-30 Sept.	Secretary and J.D. Ewart, Drapers, Newcastleton. Tel: (03873) 75257.	Spinning allowed when water is above markers at Newcastleton and Kershopelfoot Bridges. No Sunday fishing.

Water	Location	Species	Season	Permit available from	Other information
Kelhead Quarry	Hoddom & Kinmount Estate, Lockerbie	Coarse Fishing	No close season	Kelhead Bungalow, Cummertrees. Tel: Cummertrees 344.	
	Dalry	Brown Trout	1 Apr. to 30 Sept.	Ken Bridge Hotel, New Galloway. Glenkens Cafe, Dalry.	No Sunday fishing on Dalry A.A. waters. Fly only to 1 June.
Milk	Scroggs Bridge	Sea Trout Brown Trout	1 Apr. to 30 Sept.	Castle Milk Estates Office, Norwood Lockerbie. Tel: Kettleholm 203/4.	Fly fishing only. No Sunday fishing.
		Salmon Trout Coarse		Dryfesdale Hotel, Lockerbie, Dumfriesshire.	
Nith	Dumfries	Salmon Sea Trout Brown Trout	25 Feb. to 30 Nov. 15 Mar. to 6 Oct.	Director of Finance, Nithsdale District Council, Municipal Chambers, Dumfries. Tel: Dumfries 53166.	No Sunday fishing. Visitors fishing Monday to Friday only, except season ticket holders. Advance booking.
				Dumfries & Galloway Angling Association Secretary, D. Byers, 4 Bloomfield Edinburgh Road, Dumfries DG1 1SG. Tel: (0387) 53850	Limited number of permits. Weekly permits from Mon.-Fri. Advance booking possible. Spinning restrictions.
	Thornhill	Salmon Sea Trout Brown Trout	25 Feb.-30 Nov. 1 Apr. to 30 Sept.	Mid Nithsdale Angling Assoc., Secretary, Mr. I.R. Milligan, 37 Drumlanrig Street, Thornhill DG3 5LS. Tel: (0848) 30555.	No day permits on Saturdays. Spinning & worming allowed, only in flood conditions. Advisable to book for autumn fishing.
		Salmon Sea Trout Brown Trout	April to 30 Nov.	Buccleuch Estates Ltd., Drumlanrig Mains, Thornhill, Dumfriesshire DG3 4AG. Tel: (08486) 283.	Three beats - weekly lets. Two rods per beat with optional third rod. One beat-daily let-three rods. Two trout lochs with boat on each; stocked with Brook, Brown and Rainbow trout for let on daily basis exclusively up to three rods per loch.
Nith (and Tributaries Kello Crawick Euchan Mennock)	Sanquhar	Salmon Sea Trout Brown Trout Grayling	15 Mar. to 30 Nov. Jan., Feb.	Upper Nithsdale Angling Club. W. Forsyth, Solicitor, 100 High Street, Sanquhar, Dumfriesshire. Tel: Sanquhar 50241.	No Saturday/Sunday fishing. Visitors and residents. Day tickets - limit of 10 per day during months: Sept., Oct. & Nov.
Tarf	Kirkcowan	Sea Trout Brown Trout	Easter - 30 Sept.	A. Brown, Three Lochs Caravan Park, Kirkcowan, Newton Stewart, Wigtownshire. Tel: Kirkcowan 304.	
	Kirkcowan	Salmon Brown Trout Pike	18 Feb to 31 Oct.	David Canning Torwood House Hotel, Glenluce, Newton Stewart. Tel: (05813) 463.	Sunday fishing for pike only. Salmon best 1 Sep. to 31 Oct.

Water	Location	Species	Season	Permit available from	Other information
Urr	Dalbeattie	Salmon Sea Trout Brown Trout	25 Feb. to 29 Nov. 15 Mar. to 6 Oct.	Castle Douglas and District Angling Association Tommy's Sport Shop, King Street, Castle Douglas. Tel: (0556) 2861. Dalbeattie Angling Association Ticket Sec., M. McCowan & Son, 43 High Street, Dalbeattie. Tel: (0556) 610270.	
White Esk	Eskdalemuir	Salmon Sea Trout	15 Apr. to 30 Sept.	Hart Manor Hotel, Eskdalemuir, by Langholm. Tel: Eskdalemuir 73217.	Fly and spinner only.

LOCHS AND RESERVOIRS

Water	Location	Species	Season	Permit available from	Other information
Barscobe Loch	Balmaclellan	Brown Trout	15 Mar. to 6 Oct.	Sir Hugh Wontner, Barscobe, Balmaclellan, Castle Douglas. Tel: (064 42) 245/294.	
Black Esk Reservoir	Eskdalemuir	Brown Trout	1 Apr. to 30 Sept.	Hart Manor Hotel, Eskdalemuir, by Langholm. Tel: Eskdalemuir 73217.	Fly and spinner only.
Black Loch	Newton Stewart	Brown Trout (stocked)	15 Apr. to 30 Sept.	Forestry Commission, Creebridge. Tel: (0671) 2420. Galloway Deer Museum, New Galloway. Tel: (064 42) 285.	Fly only until 1 July.
Bruntis Loch	Newton Stewart	Brown/ Rainbow Trout	15 Mar. to 30 Sept.	Newton Stewart Angling Association. Galloway Guns & Tackle, Arthur Street, Newton Stewart. Tel: Newton Stewart 3404.	Bank fishing only. Sunday fishing.
Carsfad Loch	Dalry	Brown Trout	1 April to 30 Sept.	P.O. Shop, Carsphairn.	Obtain permit before fishing.
Castle Loch	Lochmaben	Bream Perch	No close season	Mr. Armstrong, Lochside Cottage, Lochmaben. Tel: Lochmaben 810340.	
		Salmon Trout Coarse		Dryfesdale Hotel, Lockerbie, Dumfriesshire.	
Clattering-shaws Loch	6 miles west of New Galloway	Trout Pike Perch	Open all year for coarse fish	Galloway Deer Museum, New Galloway. Tel: (064 42) 285.	
Dalbeattie Reservoir	Dalbeattie	Brown/ Rainbow Trout	15 Apr. to 30 Sept.	Dalbeattie Angling Association M. McCowan & Son, 43 High Street, Dalbeattie. Tel: (0556) 610270.	Bank fishing. Fly only.
Loch Dee	New Galloway	Brown Trout	15 Mar. to 6 Oct.	Forestry Commission, Creebridge. Tel: (0671) 2420 or Castle Douglas Tel: (0556) 3626. Galloway Deer Museum, New Galloway. Tel: (064 42) 285.	Fly fishing only, sunrise to sunset. No boats. Sunday fishing.

Water	Location	Species	Season	Permit available from	Other information
Dindinnie Reservoir	Stranraer	Brown Trout	15 Mar. to 30 Sept.	Stranraer & District Angling Association. The Sports Shop, 90 George Street, Stranraer. Tel: (0776) 2705. Local hotels.	Fly fishing only. Sunday fishing.
Loch Dornal	Drumlamford Estate,	Salmon Trout Coarse	Open all year	The Keeper, The Kennels, Drumlamford Estate, Barrhill. Tel: (046 582) 220.	Spinning allowed. Boats available.
Loch Drumlamford	Drumlamford Estate	Salmon Sea Trout Coarse	April to October	The Keeper, The Kennels, Drumlamford Estate, Barrhill. Tel: (046 582) 220.	Fly fishing only. Boats available.
Earlstoun Loch	Dalry	Brown Trout	1 Apr. to 30 Sept.	Glenkens Cafe, Dalry.	Fly only. Boat only. (2 boats).
Glenkiln Reservoir	Dumfries	Brown Trout (stocked) Rainbow Trout	1 Apr. to 30 Sept.	Director of Water & Sewerage, Marchmount House, Marchmount, Dumfries DG1 1PW. Tel: (0387) 61234.	
Hightae Mill Loch	Lochmaben	Bream Carp Tench Rudd Chub Roach		J. Wildman, Annandale Cottage, Greenhill, Lockerbie. Tel: Lochmaben 478.	Fishing by boat only. No restrictions.
Jericho Loch	Dumfries	Brown Trout Rainbow Trout Brook Trout	1 Apr. to 30 Sept.	Mouswald Caravan Park, Mouswald, by Dumfries. Tel: (038 783) 226. Thistle Stores, Locharbriggs. Sunday tickets from:- Tourist Information Centre, Dumfries, Tel: (0387) 53862.	Bank fishing only. Fly fishing only. Sunday fishing.
Loch Ken	West Bank Lochside Aird's (Viaduct)	Salmon Trout and coarse fish	Open all year for coarse fish	Shops, hotels in New Galloway	Surcharged if permits bought from bailiffs.
		Pike Perch	All year.	Galloway View, Balmaclellan, Castle Douglas. Tel: New Galloway 404. Local hotels.	
Kirriereoch Loch	Newton Stewart	Brown Trout	15 Mar. to 6 Oct.	Newton Stewart Angling Association. Galloway Guns & Tackle, Arthur Street, Newton Stewart. Tel: Newton Stewart 3404.	Bank fishing only. Fly fishing only. Sunday fishing.
Knockquassan Reservoir	Stranraer	Brown Trout	15 Mar. to 30 Sept.	Stranraer & District Angling Association. The Sports Shop, 90 George Street, Stranraer. Tel: (0776) 2705. Local hotels.	Bank fishing only. Fly and spinner. Sunday fishing.

Water	Location	Species	Season	Permit available from	Other information
Lairdmannoch Loch	Twynholm	Brown Trout	1 Apr. to 30 Sept.	G.M. Thomson, & Co. Ltd., 27 King Street, Castle Douglas. Tel: (0556) 2701.	Boat fishing only. Limited rods. Limited days. Self-catering Accom. Available.
Lillies Loch	New Galloway	Brown Trout	15 Mar. to 6 Oct.	Forestry Commission, Creebridge. Tel: (0671) 2420.	Bank fishing only. Any legal method. Sunday fishing.
Lochenbreck Loch	Lauriston	Brown/ Rainbow Trout	1 Apr. to 30 Sept.	Watson McKinnel, 15 St. Cuthbert Street, Kirkcudbright. Tel: (0557) 30693. M. & E. Brown, Gatehouse of Fleet, Tel: 222.	8.30 am to 10 pm. Bank fishing. Five boats. Sunday fishing.
Loch of the Lowes	Newton Stewart	Brown trout (stocked)	15 Mar. to 6 Oct.	Forestry Commission Creebridge. Tel: (0671) 2420.	Fly only. Sunday fishing.
Loch Maberry	Drumlamford Estate	Salmon Trout Coarse	Open all year	The Keeper, The Kennels, Drumlamford Estate, Barrhill. Tel: (046 582) 220.	Spinning allowed. Boats available.
Penwhirn Reservoir	Stranraer	Brown Trout	15 Mar. to 30 Sept.	Stranraer & District Angling Association. The Sports Shop, 90 George Street, Stranraer. Tel: (0776) 2705. Local hotels.	Fly fishing and spinning. Bank fishing. Sunday fishing.
Purdom Stone Reservoir	Hoddom & Kinmount Estates, Lockerbie	Brown Trout	1 Apr. to 15 Sept.	The Water Bailiff, 2 Bridge End Cottage, Hoddom, Lockerbie. Tel: Ecclefechan 488.	Fly fishing only.
Loch Roan	Castle Douglas	Brown/ Rainbow Trout	1 Apr. to 6 Oct.	Tommy's Sports Shop, King Street, Castle Douglas. Tel: (0556) 2851.	Fly fishing only. Four boats.
Soulseat Loch	Stranraer	Brown/ Rainbow Trout	15 Mar. to 30 Sept.	Stranraer & District Angling Association. The Sports Shop, 90 George Street, Stranraer. Tel: (0776) 2705. Local hotels.	Fly, spinning and bait. Bank fishing and two boats. Sunday fishing.
Loch Stroan	Castle Douglas	Pike Perch	15 May to 23 Oct.	Forestry Commission, 21 King Street, Castle Douglas. Tel: (0556) 3262. Ticket machines both ends Raiders Road Forest Drive.	Bank fishing only. Any legal method. Sunday fishing.
Torwood Lochs	Glenluce	Trout Bream Tench Carp Roach Rudd Perch	No close season	David Canning, Torwood House Hotel, Glenluce, Newton Stewart. Tel: (05813) 469.	

Water	Location	Species	Season	Permit available from	Other information
Loch Whinyeon	Gatehouse of Fleet	Brown Trout	1 Apr. to 30 Sept.	M. & E. Brown, Gatehouse of Fleet. Tel: 222.	8 am to 10 pm. Bank and fly fishing only.
Whitefield Loch	Glenluce	Pike Perch	No close season	David Canning, Torwood House Hotel, Glenluce, Newton Stewart. Tel: (05813) 469.	

DUMFRIES AND GALLOWAY
Sea Angling

Solway Firth to Mull of Galloway and Loch Ryan
An area of many headlands and off-shore reefs with strong tidal runs which can give rise to dangerous sea conditions with rising winds. Small boat anglers should always seek local advice before putting to sea. The Solway Firth area is noted for its many fine shore marks, many of which produce species such as bass, bullhuss and tope in far greater numbers than marks further north. Shore marks on the Kirkcudbrightshire coast regularly produce large cod during the winter months.

Kippford by Dalbeattie
Kippford is a well known yachting centre on the Solway Firth which offers some very good fishing, especially for flatfish.

Types of fish: Cod, flounder, plaice from the shore. Flatfish (including turbot), cod, tope, mackerel, and pollack from boats.

Bait: Lugworm can be dug locally. Cockles and mussels from the shore at low water.

Season for fishing: Best May-October. Some winter fishing for cod to 30lb.

Kirkcudbright
Kirkcudbright is a picturesque town with a very good but tidal harbour. It is approximately three miles from fishing grounds, which offer excellent tope as well as good general fishing. The coast is rugged and not recommended for dinghy or small boat fishing.

Types of fish: Cod, coalfish, conger, bass, plaice, flounders, pollack and dogfish from the shore. Cod, coalfish, conger, dogfish, mackerel, haddock, tope, pollack, all types of flatfish and whiting from the boats. Local sea angling clubs hold regular outings and competitions, where visitors are welcome. Information in Harbour Square.

Tackle: Available from W. McKinnel, 15 St. Cuthbert Street, Kirkcudbright. Patties, 109 Queensberry Street, Dumfries, Dumfriesshire. Tel: (0387) 52891.

Bait: Lugworm can be dug locally. Mussels available at low water.

Season for fishing: May- October. Some winter fishing.

Further information from: Tourist Information Centre, Tel: Kirkcudbright (0557) 30494.

Garlieston
Garlieston has a potentially good but undeveloped tidal harbour on the east side of the Machars Peninsula in Wigtownshire with several square miles of water, sheltered by the land from prevailing winds and therefore suitable for trailed and car-top dinghies. Access from the A75 Dumfries to Stranraer road is by the A714 and B7004 from Newton Stewart.

Types of fish: Mackerel, cod, pollack and coalfish from the shore. Mackerel, cod, pollack, ray, plaice, dab, flounder and coalfish from boats.

Bait: Lugworm may be dug and mussels gathered from the foreshore.

Season for fishing: June-September.

Isle of Whithorn
This picturesque old seaport on the south-west corner of Wigtown Bay has an excellent redesigned harbour with a flourishing local sailing club. It tends to be busy in summer and is a port for 'Queenie' boats. The Isle Bay itself offers nearly a mile of sheltered water in all but severe weather conditions. There are many good rock fishing marks. Tope festivals are held here twice a year, also shore and boat fishing competitions throughout the season. Local weather forecasts can be obtained from HM Coastguard Station in the centre of the village.

Types of fish: Cod, coalfish, dogfish, conger, pollack, mackerel, wrasse from the shore. Cod, rays, flatfish, spurdog, dogfish, mackerel, conger and tope from boats.

Boats: C. Mills, 14 Main Street, Isle of Whithorn, Tel: 098 85 393. W.F. McCreadie, 1 Barrhill Avenue, Newton Stewart, Tel: 0671 2466.

Tackle: Available from A. McGhie, Radio Shop, George Street, Whithorn.

Bait: Lugworm and ragworm, mussels and limpets can be gathered on the shore. Good bait can also be bought from E. McGuire, Burnside Cottage, Isle of Whithorn, at a reasonable price (order in advance).

Season for fishing: June-September.

Further information from: Mr. E.C. McGuire, Burnside Cottage, Isle of Whithorn, Wigtownshire DG8 8LN. Tel: Whithorn (098-85) 468.

Luce Bay
There are some good shore marks, namely Sandhead Sands for Flatfish, Dogfish and Bass in season, Terrally Bay for these species plus Codling, Whiting, Spurdogfish. Around East and West Tarbet bays at the Mull of Galloway good rock fishing may be had for Lesser Spotted Dogfish, Bull Huss, Spurdogfish, Conger Eels, Wrasse, Whiting, Pollack, Coalfish, Flatfish and Mackerel in season, normally from late April to December.

Boats: W. Carter, Castle Daly Angling Centre, Auchenmalg, Glenluce. Tel: 058 15 250. (Self drive boats for hire & hotel accommodation). W.F. McCreadie, 1 Barrhill Avenue, Newton Stewart, Tel: (0671) 2466.

Port William
Port William is situated on the east side of Luce Bay and has a good though tidal harbour. It is the starting point for many anglers wishing to fish the lower part of Luce Bay. The once famous shore mark of Monreith Bay, still a good bass beach, lies just to the south of Port William.

94

Types of fish: Tope, spurdog, rays, cod, pollack, flatfish from boats. Bass, wrasse, codling and pollack from the shore.

Boats: Bryce Waller, Ivy Cottage, 18 High Street, Port William, Tel: 098 87 249.

Tackle: Available in village.

Bait: Lugworm, shellfish and molluscs along beach. Mackerel in bay.

Season for fishing: May- October.

Drummore

Drummore, the main port for anglers wishing to fish the western side of Luce Bay lies 5 miles north of the Mull of Galloway. Hotels and guest houses cater for anglers. There are many good shore marks on sandy beaches north of Drummore, while the Mull of Galloway provides excellent shore fishing over rocky ground. The Mull, the most southerly part of Scotland, is an area of very strong tides and is not recommended as a fishing area to anglers with small boats incapable of at least 10 knots, especially during ebb tides.

Types of fish: Pollack, wrasse from rocky shores, flatfish, bass, mullet, porbeagle shark and rays from sandy beaches. Pollack, coalfish, cod, whiting, wrasse, lesser, spotted dogfish, bullhuss, spurdog, tope, rays, conger from boats.

Bait: All types available on shore at low tide. Mackerel from Mull of Galloway shore marks.

Port Logan

Port Logan is the small community which is situated about 7½ miles north of the Mull of Galloway on the west side of the Galloway Peninsula. An area with many good shore marks both to the north and south of the village. It is one of the few relatively easy launching sites on this coastline south of Portpatrick. A good alternative for the angler with his own boat when easterly winds prevent fishing in Luce Bay. Like the Mull of Galloway an area of strong tides, especially off Crammoc Head, to the south of Port Logan Bay.

Types of fish: As for the southern part of Luce Bay with occasional haddock. Herring in June and July.

Portpatrick

The small fishing port and holiday resort of Portpatrick lies on the west coast of Wigtownshire, 8 miles from Stranraer. There is good shore fishing from the many rocky points north and south of the resort, the best known being the Yellow Isle, ½ mile north of the harbour. Sandeel Bay, a little further north, and Killintringan Lighthouse are also worth fishing.

Types of fish: Pollack, coalfish, plaice, flounder, codling, mackerel, dogfish, conger, wrasse, and tope occasionally.

Boats: M. Wood, Ard Choille, Guest House, 1 Blair Terrace, Portpatrick, Wigtownshire. Tel: (077681) 468.

Bait: None sold locally. Lugworm and some ragworm can be dug east of the railway pier, Stranraer.

Season for fishing: May-December.

Further information from: Mr R. Smith, 24 Millbank Road, Stranraer. Tel: Stranraer (0776) 3691.

Stranraer & Loch Ryan

Stranraer, at the head of Loch Ryan, offers the angler, as a rail and bus terminal, a good stepping off point for many sea angling marks and areas in this part of Scotland, with Sandhead on Luce Bay (8 miles) to the south, Portpatrick (8 miles) to the west and Lady Bay (8 miles) on the west side of Loch Ryan with Cairnryan (6 miles) and Finnart Bay (10 miles) on the opposite side of the loch. Best Shore marks being Cairnryan Village, South of Townsend Thoresen ferry terminal. Old House Point and Concrete Barges north of Cairnryan Village, Finnart Bay on East Mouth of Loch, Wig Bay, Jamiesons Point and Lady Bay on west side of Loch Ryan. Boats may be launched at Wig Bay Slipway, Lady Bay and at Stranraer Market Street.

Types of fish: Cod, pollack, mackerel, whiting, flatfish, (Gurnard, conger, dogfish thornback and occasional tope.

Boats: Roy Ferris, Kirkcolm, Tel: (0776) 853274. Wm. McCreadie, 21 Park Road, Dunragit, Tel: 058 14 273.

Tackle: The Sports Shop, George Street, Stranraer, Tel: (0776) 2705, (frozen bait stocked).

Bait: Excellent lugworms can be dug at low tide from the sands exposed to the east side of the railway pier at low tide.

Further information from: Mr S. Dutton, "Auld Haim", Main Street, Cairnryan, Tel: 058-12-248. Mr. R. Smith, 24 Millbank Road, Stranraer, Tel: Stranraer (0776) 3691.

Constituent Area Tourist Boards

Ayrshire and Burns Country Tourist Board
Director of Tourism,
Ayrshire & Burns Country Tourist Board,
39 Sandgate, Ayr KA7 1BG.
Tel: Ayr (0292) 284196.

Ayrshire Valleys Tourist Board
Tourist Officer,
Ayrshire Valleys Tourist Board,
62 Bank Street,
Kilmarnock,
Ayrshire KA1 1ER.
Tel: Kilmarnock (0563) 39090.

Clyde Valley Tourist Board
Tourism Officer,
Clyde Valley Tourist Board,
Horsemarket,
Ladyacre Road,
Lanark ML11 7LQ.

Cunninghame District Council
Tourist Officer,
Cunninghame District Council,
Tourist Information Centre,
Largs,
Ayrshire KA30 8BG.
Tel: Largs (0475) 673765

Isle of Arran Tourist Board
Area Tourist Officer,
Isle of Arran Tourist Board,
Information Centre, The Pier,
Brodick, Isle of Arran KA27 8AU.
Tel: Brodick (0770) 2140/2401.

Greater Glasgow Tourist Board
Chief Executive,
Greater Glasgow Tourist Board,
39 St. Vincent Place,
Glasgow G1 2ER.
Tel: 041-227 4885/4880.

Other Tourist Organisations

**CUMBERNAULD AND KILSYTH
INVERCLYDE
MONKLANDS
EAST KILBRIDE
EASTWOOD**

RIVER PURIFICATION BOARD
CLYDE RIVER PURIFICATION BOARD
River House, Murray Road, East Kilbride,
Tel: East Kilbride 38181.

RIVERS

Water	Location	Species	Season	Permit available from	Other information
Annick	Irvine	Salmon Sea Trout Brown Trout	15 Mar. to 31 Oct. 15 Mar. to 6 Oct.	Dreghorn Angling Club, Mr. M. Fullerton, 12 Rigfoot Girdle Toll, Irvine, Ayrshire. Tel: Irvine 93 213072.	
Annick (and Glazert)	Kilmaurs	Salmon Sea Trout Brown Trout	15 Mar.to 31 Oct. 15 Mar. to 6 Oct.	Kilmaurs Angling Club, J. Watson, 7 Four Acres Drive, Kilmaurs or T.C. McCabe, 8 East Park Crescent, Kilmaurs.	
Avon	Strathaven	Brown Trout Grayling	15 Mar. to 6 Oct.	Sportsman Emporium, Hamilton. Country Lines, 29 Main Street, The Village, E. Kilbride. Tel: (03552) 28952. P. & R. Torbet, 15 Strand Street, Kilmarnock. Tel: (0563) 41734.	
Ayr	Mauchline	Salmon Sea Trout Brown Trout	15 Mar. to 31 Oct. 15 Mar. to 15 Sept.	Linwood & Johnstone Newsagent, The Cross, Mauchline.	

Water	Location	Species	Season	Permit available from	Other information
Ayr (Cessnock Lugar)	Mauchline	Salmon Sea Trout Brown Trout	11 Feb. to 31 Oct. 15 May-6 Oct.	Linwood & Johnstone Newsagents, The Cross, Mauchline.	
Ayr (Lugar)	Mauchline	Salmon Sea Trout Brown Trout	15 Mar. to 30 Oct. 15 Mar.-15 Sept.	Linwood & Johnstone Newsagents, The Cross, Mauchline.	
Cessnock	Mauchline	Brown Trout	15 Mar. to 15 Sept.	Linwood & Johnstone, Newsagents, The Cross, Mauchline.	
Clyde (and Douglas	Motherwell & Lanark Carstairs, Roberton & Crawford	Brown Trout Grayling	15 Mar. to 30 Sept. All year.	United Clyde Angling Protective Association, Secretary, Joseph Quigley, 39 Hillfoot Avenue, Wishaw. Permits widely available in tackle shops in Glasgow and Lanarkshire.	
Clyde	Thankerton & Roberton	Brown Trout Grayling	15 Mar. to 6 Oct. 7 Oct.-14 Mar.	B.F. Dexter, Secretary, Lamington & District Angling Improvement Association, 18 Boghall Park, Biggar. Mr. McAdam or Mr. McMahon Waterbailiffs on Wolfclyde Bridge. H. Bryden, Newsagent, High Street, Biggar.	No Sunday fishing allowed. No rod licence required. River is stocked with trout annually. Spinning with legal lures allowed from 1st May. Fly fishing at all times. Ground baiting and keep nets are not allowed.
Douglas (and Clyde)	Douglas Water	Brown Trout Grayling	15 Mar.-30 Sep. All year.	United Clyde Angling Protective Association, Secretary, Joseph Quigley, 39 Hillfoot Avenue, Wishaw. Permits widely available in tackle shops in Glasgow and Lanarkshire.	
Forth and Clyde Canal	Whole Canal	Pike Perch Roach Tench Carp	No close season	British Waterways, Rosebank House, Main Street, Camelon, Falkirk FK1 4DS. Tel: (0324) 612415.	
Garnock	Kilbirnie	Brown Trout Salmon Sea Trout	15 Mar. to 6 Oct. 15 Mar.-31 Oct.	Kilbirnie Angling Club I. Johnstone, 12 Grahamston Avenue, Glengarnock, KA14 3AF. Tel: (0505) 682154.	No Sunday fishing after July 1.
Garnock (and Lugton)	Kilwinning	Salmon Sea Trout Brown Trout	15 Mar. to 31 Oct. 15 Mar.-6 Oct.	The Craft Shop, 42 Main Street, Kilwinning. D. & J. Cairns, Newsagents, Biars Road, Kilwinning (mid-week only).	
Gryfe	Bridge of Weir	Brown Trout Salmon Sea Trout	15 Mar.-6 Oct. 15 Mar.-31 Oct.	N. Duncan, Newsagent, Main Street, Bridge of Weir.	No Saturday or Sunday fishing.
	Kilmacolm	Brown Trout	15 Mar. to 6 Oct.	Cross Cafe, Kilmacolm.	

Water	Location	Species	Season	Permit available from	Other information
Iorsa	Isle of Arran	Salmon Sea Trout Brown Trout	1 June to 15 Oct.	The Estate Office, Dougarie, Isle of Arran. Tel: (0770-84) 259.	
Irvine	Hurlford and Crookedholm	Salmon Sea Trout Brown Trout	15 Mar. to 31 Oct. 15 Mar. to 6 Oct.	P. & R. Torbet, 15 Strand Street, Kilmarnock. Tel:(0563) 41734.	
Irvine (and Annick)	Dreghorn	Salmon Sea Trout Brown Trout	15 Mar. to 31 Oct. 15 Mar.-6 Oct.	Dreghorn Angling Club. Mr. M. Fullerton, 12 Rigfoot, Girdle Toll, Irvine, Ayrshire. Tel: Irvine 93 213072.	
Irvine (and Cessnock)	Galston	Salmon Sea Trout Brown Trout	15 Mar. to 31 Oct. 15 Mar.-6 Oct.	Galston Angling Club, Sec. J. Steven, 12 Millands Road, Galston. W.& E. Pattison, Wallace Street, Galston. P. & R. Torbet, 15 Strand Street, Kilmarnock. Tel: (0563) 41734.	
Machrie	Arran	Salmon Sea Trout	1 June to 15 Oct.	Strathtay Estate Office, Strathtay, Aberfeldy, Perthsire. Tel: (0887) 20496.	No Sunday fishing. Booking: Nov.-Oct.
Stinchar	Colmonell	Salmon Sea Trout	25 Feb. to 31 Oct.	Boars Head Hotel, Colmonell. Tel: (046588) 272. Queen's Hotel, Colmonell, Tel: (046 588) 213.	

LOCHS AND RESERVOIRS

Water	Location	Species	Season	Permit available from	Other information
Loch Arklet	Stirling & Trossachs	Brown Trout	23 Mar. to 27 Sept.	Strathclyde Reg. Council, Water Department, 419 Balmore Road, Glasgow, Tel: 041-355 5333. Or on location.	Fly fishing by rowing boat only. No live bait/spinning. Rowing boats supplied. 7 days fishing.
Loch Belston	Sinclairston	Brown Trout Rainbow Trout	15 Mar.-15 Sept.	All year round Linwood & Johnstone Newsagents, The Cross, Mauchline.	Boats available.
Loch Bradan	Straiton	Brown Trout (Stocked)	15 Mar. to 6 Oct.	Forestry Commission, Straiton, Tel: (065 57) 637. Mr. R. Heaney, Tallaminnoch, Straiton. Tel: (065 57) 617.	Five Boats. Sunday fishing.
Loch Brecbowie	Straiton	Brown Trout	15 Mar. to 6 Oct.	Forestry Commission, Straiton. Tel: (065 57) 637. Mr. R. Heaney, Tallaminnoch, Straiton. Tel: (065 57) 617.	Fly fishing advised. Sunday fishing.
Castle Semple Loch	Lochwinnoch	Pike Perch Roach Eels	No close season	Rangers Centre at the loch. Tel: Lochwinnoch 842882.	Day permits for bank fishing. North shore only.

Water	Location	Species	Season	Permit available from	Other information
Glen Finglas	Stirling & Trossachs	Brown Trout	23 Mar. to 27 Sept.	Strathclyde Reg. Council, Water Department, 419 Balmore Road, Glasgow, Tel: 041-355 5333. Or on location.	Fly fishing by rowing boat only. No live bait/spinning. Rowing boats supplied. 7 days fishing.
Hillend Reservoir	Caldercruix	Brown/ Rainbow Trout	15 Mar. to 6 Oct.	Airdrie Angling Club, Roy Burgess, 21 Elswick Drive, Caldercruix, Lanarkshire. Tel: (0236) 842050.	All legal methods. Bag limit - 6 trout. Bank and boat fishing. No ground bait. Sunday fishing.
Loch Katrine	Stirling & Trossachs	Brown Trout	23 Mar. to 27 Sept.	Strathclyde Reg. Council, Water Department, 419 Balmore Road, Glasgow, Tel: 041-355 5333. Or on location.	Fly fishing by rowing boat only. No live bait/spinning. Rowing boats supplied. 7 days fishing.
Kilbirnie Loch	Kilbirnie	Brown Trout Roach	15 Mar. to 6 Oct.	Kilbirnie Angling Club, I. Johnstone, 12 Grahamston Avenue, Glengarnock KA14 3AF. Tel: (0505) 682154.	All legal methods.
Lanark Loch	Lanark	Carp Tench	No close season		
Linfern Loch	Straiton	Pike		Mr. R. Heaney, Tallaminnoch, Straiton. Tel: (065 57) 617.	Sunday fishing.
Loch Skelloch	Straiton	Brown Trout (Stocked)	15 Mar. to 6 Oct.	Mr. R. Heaney, Tallaminnoch, Stration. Tel: (065 57) 617.	Fly fishing only. Boats available. Sunday fishing.
Strathclyde Country Park Loch (and adjacent River Clyde)	Motherwell	Carp Bream Roach Pike Perch Dace	No close season	Booking Office, Strathclyde Country Park, 366 Hamilton Road, Motherwell. Tel: Motherwell 66155.	Regulations on permit. Lead-free weights recommended.
		Grayling Trout	15 Mar. to 29 Sept.		
Loch Thom and compensations 6,7 & 8	Greenock	Brown Trout	15 Mar. to 6 Oct.	Greenock & District Angling Club, Sec. J. McMurthie, 68 Cawder Crescent, Greenock. Tel: (0475) 34408. Brian Peterson, The Fishing Shop, 12 Kelly Street, Greenock. Tel: (0475) 888085. John M. Clark, Cornalees Farm. Jean Caskie, Garvocks Farm. Jimmy Rankin, Waterside Cottage, Loch Thom, Greenock.	Fly and bank fishing only.

STRATHCLYDE SOUTH
Sea Angling

Loch Ryan to Ardrossan
The angling potential of much of the coast between Loch Ryan and Girvan remains unknown, the many rocky shores, small headlands and sandy beaches probably only attracting the anglers in an exploratory mood, or those seeking solitude in pursuit of their hobby.

Girvan
Girvan has a sheltered port and is a family holiday resort. From the end of the pier good fishing can be had for fair-sized plaice and flounders. Night fishing is good for rock cod. Just one mile to the south of the town and close to the Haven Hotel lies the noted 'Horse Rock', only about 50 yards from the main Stranraer road. Access to the rock may be gained from about half-tide. Except during very high tides and during storms it is a good shore mark providing access to water of about 20 feet on the sea-side even at low tide.

Types of fish: Haddock, plaice, hake, codling, rays, flounder, whiting, and gurnard (mostly from boat).

Tackle: Available from J.H. Murray, 3 Dalrymple Street, Girvan.

Ayr
Ayr is a popular holiday town on the estuaries of the Rivers Ayr and Doon, 32 miles south-west of Glasgow. Good shore fishing can be had on the Newton Shore, north of the harbour, from the harbour jetty and from the rocky coastline at the Heads of Ayr. Boat fishing in the bay can be very productive with good catches of cod, haddock, thornbacks, spurdogs and flatfish. Tope have also been taken from around the Lady Isle.

Types of fish: Cod, mackerel, ling, plaice, dab and pollack are the main type of fish being caught in Ayr Bay over the past few year.

Tackle: Available from Games Sport, 60 Sandgate, Ayr.

Bait: Lugworm and ragworm from Ayr and Newton shore.

Prestwick
Prestwick is a pleasant seaside holiday town on the coast between Troon and Ayr. Shore fishing is best after dark. Temporary membership of Prestwick SAC can be obtained.

Types of fish: Shore – cod, flounder, plaice, dab, coalfish, dogfish and mullet. Boat – as above plus tope and rays, thornbacks and mackerel, except mullet.

Boats: J. Wilson, 27 Wallace Avenue, Barassie, Troon, Ayrshire.

Bait: Lugworm and ragworm can be dug on Prestwick shore.

Season for fishing: Shore – October-March. Boat – all year.

Troon
Troon is a popular holiday town between Ayr and Irvine with good public transport for coastal fishing points. There is good pier fishing from the harbour. Cod and flatfish can be taken at low tide from Barassie shore. Local skippers have many good marks out on the bay, with a small wreck off the Lady Isle.

Type of fish: Shore – cod, plaice, flounder, coalfish, rays, dogfish, conger, whiting, pollack. Boat – as above plus thornback, and gurnard.

Boats: There are numerous boats available. 'Dusky Maid' – Mr J. Wilson, 27 Wallace Avenue, Barassie, Troon, Ayrshire. Tel: Troon 313161. M. V. Talisman. Tel: Prestwick 76543.

Tackle: P. & R. Torbet, 15 Strand Street, Kilmarnock.

Bait: Lugworm, ragworm and mussels from shore only. Lugworm from the Barassie shore at low tide.

Season for fishing: All year.

Irvine
Irvine on the Ayrshire coast, is a rapidly developing New Town on the River Irvine. The sea is relatively shallow, with long sandy beaches. It is a good boat fishing area. Irvine was previously a very busy port, but now the river anchorage is used by a greater number of small craft. The estuary has, in the past two years come up trumps for flatfish, dabs, flounders and plaice. South of Irvine Estuary is a small island called 'The Lady Isle'. In the past year the pollack have increased not only in number but also in size. Just off this Isle pollack can be taken with ragworm on a long flowing trace. Pollack to 10 lbs., are not an unusual sight at some club matches. For cod, close inshore is best and small coloured beads are preferred to spoon and lures. The best bait by far is a cocktail of lugworm and cockle or ragworm and cockle, all of which can be obtained locally.

Types of fish: Flounder and cod from the shore. Cod, flounder, plaice, conger, haddock, ling, whiting, and coalfish.

Boats: J. Wass, 22 Templeland Road, Dalry. Tel: Dalry (029-483) 3724.

Bait: Lugworm can be dug from foreshore at low tide and mussels under wharves.

Season for fishing: All year.

Saltcoats & Ardrossan
Saltcoats with the neighbouring towns of Stevenston and Ardrossan, is situated on the Ayrshire coast 30 miles south-west of Glasgow. Shore fishing is possible in the South Bay and around the harbours. Approximately 3 miles north is Ardneil Bay which is prolific cod ground.

Types of fish: Cod, rays, flounder, coalfish, dogfish, conger, whiting and pollack from shore, plus haddock, dab, gurnard and thornback from boats.

Boats: J. Wass, 22 Templeland Road, Dalry, Tel: Dalry (029-483) 3724.

Tackle: Available from Leisure Time, 42 Hamilton Street, Saltcoats.

Bait: Limited supplies of ragworm, lugworm, sandgapers and crab are available at the tanker berth, while lugworm can be found on the north and south shores. N. Gibson can supply fresh or preserved bait.

Season for fishing: All year round from shore. March-October from boats.

Largs
Largs is within easy reach of several good fishing banks, including the Piat Shoal, the Skelmorlie Patch and the east shore of Cumbrae.

Types of fish: Dogfish, flounders, gurnard, grey sole, haddock, hake, pollack, mackerel, plaice.

Boats: Are readily available from local hirers.

Tackle: Hastie of Largs Ltd, Department Store, 109 Main Street, Largs. Tel: Largs 673104

Bait: Mussels are available from Fairlie Flats.

Gourock

The coastline from Largs to Greenock is probably the most popular area in Scotland for shore angling, with many anglers from the Midlands of England and beyond making regular trips north. At Wemyss Bay, angling is not permitted from the pier, but good catches can be had to the south, and the Red Rocks, about a mile to the north, are noted for codling and other species. At Inverkip there is a sandy beach around the entrance to the marina where large flounders and other flatfish can be taken. Cloch Point, where the Firth turns east, is well known for its fishing potential, although the current can be fierce, and because of the rough bottom, relatively heavy lines are necessary. The coastline from Cloch along Gourock Promenade to the swimming pool car park provides good fishing and is easily accessible. Further inland, at Greenock Esplanade, codling and flatfish are among the species available, although the water here is shallower, and this area is more productive at night. This stretch of coastline provides the dinghy angler with easy access to many of the Clyde marks, including the Gantocks, where outsize cod and coalfish have been taken, mainly on pirks. The bay beside the power station holds large flatfish and the ground off Greenock Esplanade is popular for codling. Dinghy owners should note that no anchoring is permitted in the main navigation channels, and several other regulations must also be adhered to.

Types of fish: Coalfish (known locally as saithe), cod, conger eel, dab, dogfish, flounder, occasional ling, plaice, pollack (lythe), pouting, whiting and wrasse. Grey mullet, herring and mackerel can also be caught during the summer months.

Tackle: K.A. Binnie, 29 Kempock Street, Gourock.

Bait: Lug, rag, mussels, cockles and crabs are easily obtainable from the shoreline.

Boats: J. Crowther, Inverclyde Boat Owners Association, 164 Burns Road, Greenock. Tel: (0475) 34341 can advise.

Isle of Arran

The island of Arran, lying in the outer Firth of Clyde, may be reached from the mainland by ferries running from Ardrossan to Brodick, the largest community on the island. Good shore fishing is found around the whole of the island, much of which remains unexplored.

Lamlash

Lamlash is the main centre for sea angling on the island, probably because of its situation on the shores of Lamlash Bay, the large horse-shoe shaped bay which is almost landlocked by the Holy Isle. This gives excellent protection to the bay from easterly winds. Lamlash is also the starting point for boat trips to the excellent fishing grounds off Whiting Bay and those around Pladda to the south.

Types of fish: Cod, haddock, whiting, coalfish, pollack, conger, rays, flatfish, mackerel, dogfish.

Bait: Obtainable from many beaches.

Season for fishing: March-November.

Corrie

Corrie is situated on north east coast of the island.

Types of fish: Cod, haddock, conger, skate, dogfish, tope, turbot, ling, pollack, gurnard and garfish.

Whiting Bay

This bay, which takes its name from the whiting, is very open to the sea. There are excellent fishing banks from Largiebeg Point to King's Cross Point.

Boats: Dinghies can be hired from the Jetty, Whiting Bay or by arrangement with Jim Ritchie, Tel: Whiting Bay (07707) 382.

Bait: Cockles, mussels, lugworm, ragworm, limpets and crabs are abundant on the banks from half-tide.

Lochranza

Lochranza is situated at the northern end of the island. The loch is surrounded by hills opening out on to Kilbrennan Sound.

Types of fish: Cod, conger, and haddock from the shore. Cod, conger, haddock from boats.

Tackle: Available from boat hirers.

Bait: Mussels, cockles, lugworm and ragworm obtainable.

Brodick

Good fishing in Brodick Bay from Markland Point to Clauchlands Point.

Types of fish: Codling, plaice and other flatfish, conger, wrasse and pollack, can be had from the shore while cod, haddock, conger, skate, dogfish, tope, turbot, ling, pollack, gurnard, garfish and other round fish can be fished from boats.

Bait: Mussels are obtainable from the rocks around Brodick Pier or may be purchased from boat hirers.

Isle of Cumbrae Millport

There is good fishing at a bank between the South East Point of Millport Bay (Farland Point) and Keppel Pier. Fintry Bay and Piat Shoal provide good sport. West of Portachur Point in about 15/20 fathoms and in Dunagoil Bay, S.W. Bute are good. Fairlie Channel directly seaward of Kelburn Castle is about 12/15 fathoms. East shore northwards about 10 fathoms line.

Types of fish: Saithe, conger, coalfish, haddock, dogfish and mackerel.

Tackle: Available locally from boat hirers.

Bait: Mussels, worms, etc. on shore. Boat hirers and local shops provide bait.

Constituent Area Tourist Boards

Dunoon and Cowal Tourist Board
Area Tourist Officer,
Dunoon and Cowal Tourist Board,
Information Centre,
7 Alexandra Parade,
Dunoon, Argyll PA23 8AB.
Tel: Dunoon (0369) 3755.

Oban, Mull and District Tourist Board
Area Tourist Officer,
Oban, Mull and District Tourist Board,
Boswell House, Argyll Square,
Oban, Argyll PA34 4AN.
Tel: Oban (0631) 63122/63059.

Mid Argyll, Kintyre and Islay Tourist Board
Area Tourist Officer,
Mid Argyll, Kintyre and Islay Tourist Board,
The Pier, Campbeltown,
Argyll PA28 6EF.
Tel: Campbeltown (0586) 52056.

Isle of Bute Tourist Board
Area Tourist Officer,
Isle of Bute Tourist Board,
The Pier, Rothesay,
Isle of Bute PA20 9AQ.
Tel: Rothesay (0700) 2151.

RIVER PURIFICATION BOARD
CLYDE RIVER PURIFICATION BOARD
Rivers House,
Murray Road,
East Kilbride.
Tel: East Kilbride 38181.

RIVERS

Water	Location	Species	Season	Permit available from	Other information
Aros	Mull	Salmon Sea Trout	End June to Mid Oct.	Tackle and Books, Main Street, Tobermory, Isle of Mull. Tel: (0688) 2336.	
Awe	Taynuilt	Salmon Sea Trout	June to Sept.	Inverawe/Taynuilt Fisheries, Argyll. Tel: (08662) 446.	Rod hire. Casting tuition.
Bellart	Mull	Salmon Sea Trout	June to End Oct.	Tackle & Books, Main Street, Tobermory, Isle of Mull. Tel: (0688) 2336.	No Sunday fishing.
Cur	13 miles from Dunoon	Salmon Sea Trout Brown Trout	1 Apr. to 31 Oct.	Purdies of Argyll, 112 Argyll Street, Dunoon. Tel: Dunoon 3232. Dunoon & District Angling Club.	Fishing all legal methods. Bookings, Hon. Sec. D. & D.A.C., 7 Blair Lane, Stewart Street, Dunoon. Tel: Dunoon 5732.
Douglas	Inveraray	Salmon Sea Trout	May to Mid-Oct.	Argyll Caravan Park, Inveraray, Argyll. Tel: (0499) 2285.	No Sunday fishing. Fly fishing only.
Euchar	Kilninver	Salmon Sea Trout Brown Trout	1 June to 15 Oct.	Mrs. Mary McCorkindale, 'Glenann' Kilninver, by Oban, Argyll. Tel: Kilninver 282.	No Sunday fishing.
		Salmon Sea Trout	Mid-July to Mid-Oct.	J.T.P. Mellor, Barncromin Farm, Knipoch, by Oban, Argyll. Tel: Kilninver 273.	(Tues, Wed & Thurs.)
	Kilninver (Lagganmore)	Salmon Sea Trout Brown Trout	June to 14 Oct.	Lt. Col. P.S. Sandilands, Lagganmore, Kilninver, by Oban. Tel: Kilninver 200.	Not more than 3 rods per day. Charges: £3 per rod, per day. Fly fishing only. No Sunday fishing.

Water	Location	Species	Season	Permit available from	Other information
Finnart	12 miles from Dunoon	Salmon Sea Trout Brown Trout	1 Apr. to 15 Oct.	Dunoon & District Angling Club. Purdie's of Argyll, 112 Argyll Street, Dunoon. Tel: Dunoon 3232.	Fishing all legal methods. Advanced bookings Hon. Sec. D.&D.A.C., 7 Blair Lane, Stewart Street, Dunoon. Tel: Dunoon 5732.
Forsa	Mull	Salmon Sea Trout	Mid-June to Mid-Oct.	Tackle and Books, Main Street, Tobermory. Tel: (0688) 2336.	No Sunday fishing.
		Salmon Sea Trout	Early July to Mid-Oct.	Glenforsa Hotel, by Salen. Tel: (06803) 00377.	No Sunday fishing.
Goil	Lochgoilhead	Salmon Sea Trout	May to End-Oct.	R. Kennedy, Drumsyniebeg, Lochgoilhead. Tel: (03013) 272.	No Sunday Fishing. No spinning.
Machrie	Islay	Salmon Sea Trout	25 Feb. to 31 Oct.	Machrie Hotel, Port Ellen, Islay, Argyll PA42 7AN. Tel: (0496) 2310.	Own river.
Massan	6 miles from Dunoon	Salmon Sea Trout Brown Trout	1 Apr. to 31 Oct.	Dunoon & District Angling Club. Purdies of Argyll, 112 Argyll Street, Dunoon. Tel: Dunoon 3232.	All legal methods. Advanced booking Hon. Sec. D. & D.A.C., 7 Blair Lane, Stewart Street, Dunoon. Tel: Dunoon 5732.
Orchy	Dalmally	Salmon	11 Feb. to 15 Oct.	W.A. Church, Croggan Crafts, Dalmally, Argyll. Tel: Dalmally 201.	
Ruel	Glendaruel	Salmon Sea Trout	16 Feb. to 31 Oct.	Glendaruel Hotel, Clachan of Glendaruel, Argyll PA22 3AA. Tel: (036982) 274.	No Sunday fishing.

LOCHS AND RESERVOIRS

Water	Location	Species	Season	Permit available from	Other information
Loch Ascog	Argyll	Brown/ Rainbow Trout	15 Mar. to 5 Oct.	Kyles of Bute Angling Club. Several shops in Kames and Tighnabruaich.	Fly only.
Loch Assopol	Mull	Salmon Sea Trout	April to beg. Oct.	Argyll Arms Hotel, Bunessan, Isle of Mull. Tel: Fionnphort 240.	Fly and spinner only. No Sunday fishing.
Loch Avich	Taynuilt	Brown Trout Rainbow Trout	15 Mar. to 6 Oct.	Fleming, 35 Dalavich, By Taynuilt, Argyll PA35 1HN. Tel: Lochavich 230.	
Loch Awe	Taynuilt	Salmon Sea Trout Brown Trout Rainbow Trout	12 Feb. to 15 Oct. 15 Mar. to 6 Oct.	Fleming, 35 Dalavich, By Taynuilt, Argyll PA35 1HN. Tel: Lochavich 230.	

Water	Location	Species	Season	Permit available from	Other information
Loch Awe contd.		Sea Trout Brown Trout Salmon Pike Perch Char	12 Feb.-15 Oct. 15 Mar.-6 Oct.	Forestry Commission, Loch Awe Forest District, Whitegates, Lochgilphead, Tel: Lochgilphead 2518. Mrs. Stewart, Tel: Lochavich 211.	
	Ford	Brown Trout	15 Mar. to 6 Oct.	Ford Hotel, Ford, Argyll. Tel: (054 681) 273.	
	South Lochaweside Nr. Dalmally	Salmon Brown Trout Sea Trout Rainbow Trout Pike Perch Char	15 Mar.-15 Oct. 15 Mar.-6 Oct.	The Portsonachan Hotel, Nr.Dalmally, Argyll PA33 1BL. Tel: (086 63) 224/225/356/328.	
	Dalmally	Salmon Sea Trout Brown Trout Rainbow Trout Pike	11 Feb. to 15 Oct. 15 Mar.-6 Oct. All year.	Ardbrecknish House, by Dalmally, Argyll. Tel: (08663) 223.	Self Catering flats. Rods, tackle & ghillie available. Boats.
Barnluasgan Loch	Lochgilphead	Brown Trout	15 Mar. to 6 Oct.	Mrs. Robertson, Barnluasgan, Lochgilphead.	One boat.
Coille Bhar	Lochgilphead	Brown Trout	1 Apr. to 6 Oct.	Mrs. Robertson, Barnluasgan, Lochgilphead.	Two boats
Dubh Loch	Kilninver	Loch Leven Trout Brown Trout	April to Mid-Oct.	J.T.P. Mellor, Barndromin Farm, Knipoch, by Oban. Tel: Kilninver 273.	Boat on loch.
Dunoon Reservoir	Dunoon	Rainbow & Brook Trout	1 Mar. to 31 Nov.	Dunoon & District Angling Club. Purdies of Argyll, 112 Argyll Street, Dunoon. Tel: Dunoon 3232.	Fly fishing only.
Loch Fad	Bute	Brown Trout Rainbow Trout	29 Mar. to 30 Sept.	Bailiff at Loch. Tel: (0700) 4871.	Boats available. Whole day and evening tickets. No night fishing.
		Rainbow Trout Brown Trout	April to October	Carleol Enterprises Angling Holidays, 3 Alma Terrace, Rothesay. Tel: (0700) 3716.	Accommodation and permits are available.
Loch Finlaggan	Islay	Brown Trout	15 Mar. to 30 Sept.	Brian Wiles, Islay House Square, Bridgend, Isle of Islay, Argyll PA44 7NZ. Tel: (049 681) 293.	Two boats.
Loch Gleann A'Bhearraidh	Lerags by Oban	Brown Trout	15 Mar. to 6 Oct.	Cologin Homes Ltd., Lerags, by Oban, Argyll. Tel: Oban 64501. The Barn Bar, Cologin, Lerags, by Oban.	One boat available.

Water	Location	Species	Season	Permit available from	Other information
Loch Gorm	Islay	Brown Trout	15 Mar. to 30 Sept.	Brian Wiles, Islay House Square, Bridgend, Isle of Islay, Argyll PA44 7NZ. Tel: (049 681) 293.	3 Boats available.
Inverawe Fisheries	Taynuilt	Rainbow Trout	Mar. to Nov.	Inverawe Fisheries, Taynuilt, Argyll. Tel: (08662) 446.	
Kilmelford Lochs	Kilmelford	Brown Trout		Oban & Lorne Angling Club.	Numerous Lochs
Lochgilphead Lochs	Lochgilphead	Brown Trout	15 Mar. to 6 Oct.	Lochgilphead and District Angling Club. The Sports Shop, Lochnell Street, Lochgilphead.	Numerous lochs. No Sunday fishing.
Lochquien	Bute	Brown Trout	1 Apr. to 6 Oct.	Bute Estate Office, Rothesay, Isle of Bute. Tel: Rothesay 2627.	Fly only. Salmon and trout fishing in sea around Bute.
Loch Loskin	1 mile from Dunoon	Brown/ Sea Trout	1 Apr. to 30 Sept.	Dunoon & District Angling Club. Purdies of Argyll, 112 Argyll Street, Dunoon. Tel: Dunoon 3232.	Fly only. Boat only.
Loch Lussa	Campbeltown	Brown Trout	15 Mar. to 6 Oct.	MacGrory & Co., 16/20 Main Street, Campbeltown. Tel: (0586) 52132.	
Mishnish & Aros Lochs	Mull	Brown Trout	15 Mar. to 30 Sept.	Tobermory Angling Association. Brown's Shop, Tobermory. Tel: (0688) 2020.	No Sunday fishing.
Loch Nell	Oban	Brown Trout	15 Mar. to 6 Oct.	Oban & Lorne Angling Club.	
Powderworks Reservoir	Argyll	Brown/ Rainbow Trout	15 Mar. to 5 Oct.	Kyles of Bute Angling Club. Several shops in Kames and Tighnabruaich.	Fly and bait only, no spinning.
Loch Scammadale	Kilninver	Salmon Sea Trout Brown Trout	1 June to 15 Oct. 15 Mar.-6 Oct.	Mrs. McCorkindale 'Glenann', Kilninver, by Oban, Argyll. Tel: Kilninver 282.	No Sunday fishing.
Loch Seil	Kilninver	Sea Trout Brown Trout	Apr. to Mid-Oct.	J.T.P. Mellor, Barndromin Farm, Knipoch, by Oban, Argyll. Tel: Kilninver 273.	Boat on Loch.
Loch Squabain	Mull	Salmon Sea Trout Brown Trout		Tackle & Books, Main Street, Tobermory, Mull. Tel: (0688) 2336.	Boat fishing only.

Water	Location	Species	Season	Permit available from	Other information
Loch Tarsan	8 miles from Dunoon	Brown Trout	1 Apr. to 30 Sept.	Dunoon & District Angling Club. Purdies of Argyll, 112 Argyll Street, Dunoon. Tel: Dunoon 3232.	Fly only
Tighnabruaich Reservoir	Tighnabruaich	Brown Trout	15 Mar. to 5 Oct.	Kyles of Bute Angling Club. Several shops in Kames and Tighnabruaich, Argyll.	
Torr Loch	North end of Mull	Wild Brown Trout Sea Trout Some Rainbow	April to Oct.	Tackle and Books, Main Street, Tobermory, Mull. Tel: (0688) 2336.	No Sunday fishing. 2 boats. Banks clear.

STRATHCLYDE NORTH

Sea Angling
Isle of Bute Rothesay
The holiday resort of Rothesay, situated on the island of Bute, only a 30 minute crossing by roll-on/ roll-off ferry from Wemyss Bay, is sheltered from the prevailing south-westerly winds. Several boat hirers cater for sea anglers. There are also many excellent shore marks. The deep water marks at Garroch Head can be productive for both shore and boat anglers.

Types of fish: Shore – cod, coalfish, pollack, plaice, mackerel, wrasse. Boat – cod, pollack, plaice, mackerel, conger, spurdog, coalfish, wrasse and whiting.

Tackle: Available from Bute Arts & Tackle, 94- 96 Montague Street, Rothesay, Isle of Bute, Tel: (0700) 3598.

Bait: Bute Arts & Tackle, 94-96 Montague Street, Rothesay, Isle of Bute, Tel: (0700) 3598. Low water at Port Bannatyne for cockles, Lugworm and ragworm. Herring is also useful bait. Mussel bait can be obtained on shore.

Season for fishing: May-October.

Kilchattan Bay
Sheltered bay waters at the south end of the Isle of Bute renowned for its good all year round fishing.

Types of fish: Cod, pollack, plaice, mackerel, conger, dogfish, wrasse, whiting.

Bait: Worm, fresh cockle available locally.

Season for fishing: All year.

Mainland Ardentinny
Ardentinny is a small unspoiled village picturesquely situated on the west shore of Loch Long, 12 miles from Dunoon by car.

Types of fish: Cod, conger, haddock, from the shore. Cod, conger, haddock, ray, plaice, flounder, whiting, coalfish and mackerel from boats.

Bait: Cockles. mussels, lug and ragworm easily dug in bay.

Season for fishing: All year, winter for large cod.

Dunoon
Types of fish:
Most of the shoreline around Dunoon provides catches of cod, coalfish, pollack, flounder, mackerel, plaice. Using ragworm & lugworm, cockle, mussel, razorfish & Peeler crab. Boat fishing takes mostly cod, pollack, coalfish, dogfish, dabs, plaice, flounder. Also conger over wrecks or rough ground at night.

Winter fishing: Also produces fair sized cod. Also haddock and whiting. So anglers can fish all year round from boat or shore.

Boats: Gourock skippers fish Dunoon waters. Approx. 3 miles from Dunoon is Holy Loch.

Tackle: Argyll Marine Sports, 60 Argyll Street, Dunoon; Purdies Fishing Tackle & Sports, 112 Argyll Street, Dunoon. Tel: Dunoon (0369) 3232.

Bait: Can be bought at these shops most of the year or obtained in East Bay shore.

Tighnabruaich & Kames
Tighnabruaich, on the Kyles of Bute, is famed for its beauty and Highland scenery. Access to some good fishing banks on the west side of the Bute and around Inchmarnock.

Types of fish: Mackerel and coalfish from the shore. Cod, haddock, flatfish, whiting, dogfish, pollack, gurnard and several species of wrasse. Conger fishing can be arranged. The winter run of big cod is well known, haddock and whiting are also caught.

Bait: Supplies of fresh bait (lug, cockle, mussel, clams etc.) are locally available.

Boats: Motor dinghies available for hire. Local fishermen can take parties of anglers by arrangement. Contact: Andy Lancaster, Kames Hotel, Tel: (0700) 811489.

Season: Spring to Autumn, plus winter cod.

Loch Fyne
This is the longest sea-loch in Scotland, penetrating into the Highlands from the waters of the lower Firth of Clyde. The depth of the water within the loch varies enormously with depth of around 100 fathoms being found not only at the seaward end but also at the head of the loch of Inveraray. Much of the shore angling potential remains unknown although access to both shores is made relatively easy by roads running down each side. Boat launching facilities are less easy to find because of the rugged shoreline. Best side is Inveraray to Furnace. Quarry is now out of bounds.

Types of fish: Mackerel, cod, pollack, flatfish, conger (at night).

Inveraray
Inveraray stands on its west shore near the head of Loch Fyne.

Types of fish: Cod, mackerel, pollack, coalfish, ling, dogfish, conger eel, hake and plaice.

Bait: Mussels and worms available from shore at low tide.

Season for fishing: June-September.

Tarbert (Loch Fyne)
The sheltered harbour and the adjacent coast of the loch near the lower end of the loch on the west shore are good fishing grounds for the sea angler.

Types of fish: Cod, mackerel, coalfish, and sea trout from the shore. Mackerel, cod, coalfish, rays, haddock and whiting from boats.

Boats: Evening out with the boats of the herring fleet can be arranged.

Tackle: Local shops.

Bait: There is an abundance of shellfish and worms on the mud flats.

Season for fishing: June, July and August.

Oban

Good catches can be occasionally taken in Kerrera Sound near the Cutter Rock and the Ferry Rocks. Fishing is much better off the south and west coasts of Kerrera Island, particularly near the Bach Island and Shepherds Hat, Maiden Island and Oban Bay give good mackerel fishing in July and August. These places are very exposed and should only be attempted in good settled weather.

Types of fish: Boat – mackerel, dogfish, rays, pollack and occasionally cod and haddock. Heavy catches (mainly dogfish) have been taken in the entry to Loch Feochan during the past two seasons.

Tackle: David Graham, 9 Combie Street, Oban.

Bait: Mussels and lugworm, etc. can be dug from the Kerrera beaches.

Season for fishing: May-November.

Sea Life Centre

11 miles north of Oban on A828. Underwater observatory for seals and other fascinating sea creatures and fish. Ideal viewing conditions. Restaurant.

Isle of Islay

This is the southernmost of the islands. Several of the larger communities like Port Ellen and Port Askaig have good harbours.

Types of fish: Boat – cod, haddock, whiting, mackerel, dogfish, flounder, conger, skate.

Tackle: available from Mr. Hodkinson, The Square, Bowmore; Mini-market, Bruichladdich; J. Campbell, sub-Post Office, Bridgend; Iain Laurie, The Bakery, Port Ellen.

Bait: Lugworm plentiful on most beaches. Clam skirts from fish factory waste. Bait can be purchased from fishing boats at the piers.

Season for fishing: All year.

Isle of Mull (Salen)

Salen is situated on the east coast of Mull facing the Sound of Mull in a central position, 11 miles from Craignure and 10 miles from Tobermory. The village is sited between Aros River and a headland forming Salen Bay. The Sound of Mull is on the main skate marks in the Argyll area. Over twenty 100 lbs., plus skate have now been taken. One of the contributing factors is the sheltered nature of the Sound, which can allow practically uninterrupted angling. This area has also yielded a number of fine tope, the largest of which was a specimen of 50 lbs. It is worth noting that cod and haddock seldom frequent the sound and should not be expected. This is an area recommended for dinghy owners.

Types of fish: Coalfish, pollack, cod, wrasse, flounder, mullet sea trout, and mackerel from the shore. Ray, skate, ling, pollack, coalfish, cod, spurdog, tope, conger and gurnard from boats.

Tackle: Available from the Tackle and Books, Main Street, Tobermory, 10 miles away.

Bait: Easily obtainable from shoreline. Mackerel bait from Tackle and Books.

Season for fishing: March-November.

Further information from: Mr. Duncan Swinbanks, Tackle and Books, 10 Main Street, Tobermory. Tel: Tobermory 2336.

Isle of Mull (Tobermory)

The principal town on Mull, it is situated on a very sheltered bay at the north eastern tip of the island. Apart from hitting the headlines in the national press with its treasure, Tobermory has been extensively covered in the angling press. It is the undisputed centre for skate fishing in 1985 and 86 claims for both British and World records were made. The largest fish captured was a giant of 227 lbs. Every year an average of 50 ton-up specimens are caught, tagged and returned alive. It is this thoughtful conservation that has maintained the quality of fishing in the area. Large tope of between 35 lbs., and 45 lbs., can be numerous. Nine Scottish records, red gurnard,

grey gurnard, blonde ray, spotted ray, spurdogfish, angler fish, turbot and two wrasse, have come from these Mull waters. Every year dramatic catches of migratory fish can be made. Coalfish, whiting, haddock and cod may be encountered on a vast scale.

Types of fish: Tope, skate, rays, pollack, coalfish, ling, conger, gurnard, spurdog, cod, haddock, flatfish (plaice, dabs, and turbot) and whiting from boats. Coalfish, pollack, cod, wrasse, flounder, grey mullet, sea trout, conger, thornback and mackerel from the shore.

Boats: Mr. Brian Swinbanks, 8 Main Street, Tobermory, has a purpose built 38 ft. sea angling boat for fishing parties with boat rods and reel available. There are 14-16 ft. dinghies for hire for fishing in and around the bay.

Tackle: A tackle shop, with a complete range of stock is on the Main Street.

Bait: Herring and mackerel available from Tackle and Books, Tobermory. Mussels and lugworms are easily obtainable from the shoreline.

Season for fishing: May-November.

Further information from: Mr. Duncan Swinbanks, Tackle and Books, 10 Main Street, Tobermory. Tel: Tobermory 2336.

Isle of Coll

Coll is one of the smaller islands seaward of Mull. Fishing vessels concentrate on the Atlantic side, but good sport can be had on the Mull side and even at the mouth of Arinagour Bay where the village and hotel lie and the mail steamer calls. Fishing from rocks at several spots round the island can give good results.

Types of fish: Mackerel, coalfish, pollack, cod, conger, haddock, skate and flounder.

Boats: Dinghies with or without outboard engines can be hired from local lobster fishermen.

Tackle: Visitors are advised to bring their own.

Bait: Mussels, worms and small crabs can readily be obtained at low tide in Arinagour Bay.

Season for fishing: May to September and later depending on weather.

Constituent Area Tourist Organisations

City of Edinburgh District Council
Director,
Department of Public Relations & Tourism,
The City of Edinburgh District Council,
Waverley Market,
3 Princes Street,
Edinburgh EH2 2QP.
Tel: 031-557 2727/1700.

Forth Valley Tourist Board
Tourist Officer,
Forth Valley Tourist Board,
Burgh Hall, The Cross,
Linlithgow,
West Lothian EH49 7AH.
Tel: (0506) 84 3306.

Loch Lomond, Stirling and Trossachs Tourist Board
Tourism Manager,
Loch Lomond, Stirling and Trossachs
Tourist Board,
41 Dumbarton Road,
Stirling FK8 2LQ.
Tel: Stirling (0786) 70945.

St. Andrews and North East Fife Tourist Board
Tourism Manager,
St. Andrews and North East Fife Tourist
Board,
2 Queens Gardens, St. Andrews,
Fife KY16 9TE.
Tel: St. Andrews (0334) 74609.

Kirkcaldy District Council
Tourist Officer,
Kirkcaldy District Council,
Information Centre,
South Street, Leven,
Fife KY8 4PF.
Tel: Leven (0333) 29464.

East Lothian Tourist Board
Tourism Director,
East Lothian Tourist Board,
Brunton Hall,
Musselburgh, EH21 6AE.
Tel: 031-665 3711.

Other Tourist Organisations
MIDLOTHIAN

RIVER PURIFICATION BOARD
FORTH RIVER PURIFICATION BOARD
Colinton Dell House,
West Mill Road, Colinton,
Edinburgh EH11 0PH.
Tel: 031-441 4691.

RIVERS

Water	Location	Species	Season	Permit available from	Other information
Allan	Bridge of Allan	Salmon Sea Trout Brown Trout	15 Mar. to 31 Oct. 15 Mar. to 6 Oct.	D. Crockart & Son, King Street, Stirling. Tel: (0786) 73443.	No. Sat. or Sun. tickets after 31st July.
Almond	Cramond	Salmon Sea Trout Brown Trout	1 Feb. to 31 Oct. 15 Mar. to 6 Oct.	Cramond Angling Club. Post Office, Cramond, Edinburgh. Country Life, Balgreen Road, Edinburgh. Post Office, Davidsons Mains, Edinburgh. Shooting Lines, Roseburn Terr & Hope Park Terr., Edinburgh.	Mouth to Old Cramond Brig. East bank only.
	West Lothian	Salmon Sea Trout Brown Trout	1 Feb. to 31 Oct. 15 Mar. to 6 Oct.	River Almond Angling Association, Secretary: Mr. Craig Campbell, 2 Canmore Street, South Queensferry. Tel: 031 331 1514. Livingston Sports, Almondvale Centre, Livingston. Country Life, Balgreen Road, Edinburgh. Shooting Lines, Roseburn Terr. & Hope Park Terr., Edinburgh.	20 miles of river.

Water	Location	Species	Season	Permit available from	Other information
Devon	Dollar	Salmon Sea Trout Brown Trout	15 Mar. to 31 Oct. 15 Mar. to 6 Oct.	Devon Angling Association, R. Breingan, 33 Redwell Pl., Alloa. Tel: Alloa 215185. Scobbie Sports, 2/4 Primrose Street, Alloa. Tel: (0259) 722661. D.W. Black, The Hobby & Model Shop, 10-12 New Row, Dunfermline. Tel: (0383) 722582. D. Crockart & Son, 47 King Street, Stirling. Tel: (0786) 734433.	No Sunday fishing. Devonside Bridge upstream with excluded stretches. Fly fishing only from 15 Mar.-12 Apr.
Eden (and Ceres Burn)	Cupar	Salmon Sea Trout Brown Trout	15 Mar. to 6 Oct.	D.W. Black, The Hobby & Model Shop, 10-12 New Row, Dunfermline. Tel: (0383) 722582.	No Sunday fishing.
Endrick	Drymen	Salmon Sea Trout Brown Trout	11 Feb. to 31 Oct. 15 Mar. to 6 Oct.	Loch Lomond Angling Improvement Association. R.A. Clement & Co. C.A., 29 St. Vincent Place, Glasgow. Tel: 041-221-0068.	Members only. No Sunday fishing. No worm fishing. Spinning restricted.
Esk	Musselburgh	Salmon Sea Trout Brown Trout	1 Feb. to 31 Oct. 15 Mar. to 6 Oct.	Givan Shop, 67 Eskside West, Musselburgh. Tel: 031-665 3371.	No Sunday fishing. Regulations on permit.
Esk (North and South)	Midlothian	Brown Trout Rainbow Trout	15 Mar to 6 Oct.	Esk Valley Angling Improvement Association. Kevin Burns, 53 Fernieside Crescent, Edinburgh. Tel: 031-664 4685.	Fly rod and reel only to be used. Regulations on permit. Sunday fishing.
Forth	Stirling	Salmon Sea Trout Brown Trout	1 Feb.-31 Oct. 15 Mar. to 6 Oct.	D. Crockart & Son, 47 King Street, Stirling. Tel: (0786) 73443.	
Forth and Clyde Canal	Castlecary	Perch Pike Carp Roach Tench Bream	No close season	British Waterways Rosebank House, Main Street, Camelon, Falkirk FK1 4DS. Tel: (0324) 612415.	
Fruin	Helensburgh	Salmon Sea Trout Brown Trout	11 Feb. to 31 Oct. 1 Mar. to 6 Oct.	Loch Lomond Angling Improvement Association. R.A. Clement & Co. C.A., 29 St. Vincent Place, Glasgow. Tel: 041-221-0068.	Members only. Fly fishing only.
Water of Leith	Edinburgh	Brown Trout	1 Apr. to 30 Sept.	Post Office, 36 Main Street, Balerno. Post Office, Colinton.	Fly fishing above Slateford Road Bridge. No spinning. Regulations on permit.
Leven	Dumbarton	Salmon Sea Trout Brown Trout	11 Feb. to 31 Oct. 15 Mar. to 6 Oct.	Loch Lomond Angling Improvement Association. R.A. Clement & Co. C.A., 29 St. Vincent Place, Glasgow. Tel: 041-221-0068. Various local tackle shops.	Members may fish all Association waters. No Sunday fishing. Permits available.

Water	Location	Species	Season	Permit available from	Other information
Teith	Callander	Salmon	1 Feb. to 31 Oct.	J. Bayne, Main Street, Callander. Tel: (0877) 30218.	
	Stirling (Blue Banks)	Salmon Sea Trout	1 Feb. to 31 Oct.	D. Crockart & Son, 47 King Street, Stirling, Tel: (0786) 73443.	
Tyne	Haddington	Brown Trout Rainbow Trout	15 Mar. to 6 Oct.	East Lothian Angling Association. J.S. Main, Saddlers, 87 High Street, Haddington.	Twenty miles of river. No Sunday fishing. No threadlines. No spinning.
Union Canal	Edinburgh to Falkirk	Pike Perch Roach Carp Tench	No close season	Tourist Office, Linlithgow.	Regulations on permit.

LOCHS AND RESERVOIRS

Water	Location	Species	Season	Permit available from	Other information
Loch Achray	Callander	Brown Trout Perch Pike	15 Mar. to 6 Oct.	Forestry Commission, David Marshall Lodge, Aberfoyle. Loch Achray Hotel, Trossachs. Bayne's Fishing Tackle Shop, Callander.	Bank fishing only.
Ballo Reservoir	Lomond Hills	Brown Trout	1 Apr. to 30 Sept.	Details from: Mr. T. Duffy, Wester Glasslee, Leslie, Fife.	Fly fishing only. No Sunday fishing. No bank fishing.
Beecraigs Loch	Linlithgow	Brown Trout Rainbow Trout Brook Trout	15 Mar. to 31 Oct.	Beecraigs Country Park. Tel: Linlithgow 844516.	Fly fishing only.
Bonaly Reservoir	Edinburgh	Brown/ Rainbow Trout	1 Apr. to 30 Sept.	None Required.	
Bowden Springs	Linlithgow	Rainbow/ Brown Trout	3 Jan. to 23 Dec.	W. Martin, Bowden Springs Fishery, Linlithgow. Tel: Linlithgow 847269.	Bank and boat fishing. Fly fishing only. Minimum size 1 lb.
Cameron Reservoir	St. Andrews	Brown Trout	Mid-Apr. to End-Sept.	St. Andrews Angling Club, Secretary, Mr. P. Malcolm, 54 St. Nicholas Street, St. Andrews. Tel: (0334) 76347.	Fly fishing only. No Sunday fishing. Three rods per boat. Pre-season bookings to Secretary.
Carron Valley Reservoir	Denny	Brown Trout	16 Apr. to 22 Sept.	Director of Finance, Central Regional Council, Viewforth, Stirling. Tel: (0786) 73111.	Boat fishing only.
Loch Coulter	Nr. Carronbridge	Brown/ Rainbow Trout	1 Apr. to 30 Sept.	Larbert & Stenhousemuir Angling Club, Mrs. Shaw, Sauchie Filters. Tel: (0786) 812434.	No Sunday fishing. Fly fishing only. Day - 9 am-Dusk Evening - 6 pm-Dusk.
Crosswood Reservoir	West Calder	Brown Trout Brook Trout Rainbow Trout	1 Apr. to 30 Sept.	Dept. of Water & Drainage, Lomond House, Livingston. Tel: Livingston 414004.	Three boats. Fly fishing only.

Water	Location	Species	Season	Permit available from	Other information
Danskine Loch	Gifford	Roach Perch Carp Crucian Carp	1 Mar. to 20 Oct.	Edinburgh Coarse Anglers, Sec., R. Woods, 23 Terregles, Penicuik. Tel: (0968) 74792.	Strictly members only.
Loch Doine	Balquhidder	Salmon Brown Trout	15 Mar. to 6 Oct.	C.M Oldham & I.T. Emslie, Muirlaggan, Balquhidder, Lochearnhead FK19 8PB. Tel: (08774) 219.	Boats. Two caravans with free fishing. Weekly bookings only.
Loch Drunkie	Aberfoyle	Brown Trout	15 Mar. to 6 Oct.	Forestry Commission David Marshall Lodge, Aberfoyle. Bayne's Fishing Tackle Shop, Callander.	Bank fishing only.
Duddingston Loch	Edinburgh	Carp Perch	No close season	Historic Buildings & Monuments, 20 Brandon Street, Edinburgh. Tel: 031-244 3085.	Bird Sanctuary. Bank fishing. Restricted area. No lead weights.
Loch Fitty	Dunfermline	Brown/ Rainbow Trout	1 Mar. to Xmas	Mr. Mackenzie, The Lodge, Loch Fitty, Kingseat by Dunfermline, Fife. Tel: (0383) 723162.	Boat and Bank fly fishing. Day - 10am-5pm. Evenings - 5.30pm-dark. Reductions for single anglers, and 'Father & schoolboy Son'. Boats.
Loch Glow	Cleish Hills, Nr. Kelty	Brown Trout	15 Mar. to 6 Oct.	Mr. Balfour, Lochornie Cottage. Tackle shops in Dunfermline, Cowdenbeath, Kelty & Kinross.	Fly, bait & spinning. Regularly stocked with brown trout; some tagged fish. Further information Mr. J.W. Mill, Tel: (0383) 722128.
Harperrig Reservoir	West Calder	Brown Trout	1 Apr. to 30 Sept.	Dept. of Water & Drainage, Lomond House, Livingston, Tel: Livingston 414004. Bank fishing permits from machine at reservoir.	Correct coins required for machine, 50p 10p 5p denominations. Four boats and bank fishing. No Sunday fishing. Fly fishing only.
Lindores Loch	Newburgh	Brown/ Rainbow Trout	15 Mar. to 30 Nov.	F.G.A. Hamilton, Kindrochet Fish Farm, St. Fillans PH6 2JZ. Tel: St. Fillans 337.	Two sessions.
Linlithgow Loch	Linlithgow	Brown/ Rainbow Trout	15 Mar. to 6 Oct.	Lothian Sports Regent Centre, Linlithgow. Tel: Linlithgow 845730. For Forth Area Federation of Anglers.	Fly fishing only. Sessions: (May to Aug.) Day: 9.00 - 4.30 Evening: 5.00 - dusk Sunday: 1.00 - dusk.
Lochore	Ballingry	Brown Trout	15 Mar. to 5 Oct.	Hobby & Model Shop, Dunfermline. Sports Shop, High Street, Cowdenbeath. Lochore Meadows Country Park, Crosshill, Lochgelly, Fife. Tel. (0592) 860086.	Reductions for clubs and groups. Sessions: Day - 9 am-5 pm. Evening - 5 pm-dusk. Fly fishing and spinning. Bait fishing from bank from 1 July.

Water	Location	Species	Season	Permit available from	Other information
Loch Lomond	Balloch to Ardlui	Salmon Sea Trout Brown Trout Pike Roach Perch	11 Feb. to 31 Oct. 15 Mar.-6 Oct. No close season	Loch Lomond Angling Improvement Association R.A. Clement & Co, C.A., 29 St. Vincent Place, Glasgow. Tel: 041-221-0068. Local hotles, shops & tackle dealers	Permits cover all Association waters. Boats for hire locally. No Sunday fishing.
Maltings Fishery	West Barns, Dunbar	Brown/ Rainbow Trout	All year for Rainbow.	Dunbar Trout Farm, Tel: (0368) 63244. (Or at the fishery).	Fly only. Maximum fly size no. 10 long shank.
Morton Fishery	Mid Calder	Brown/ Rainbow Trout	9 Mar. to 2 Nov.	Morton Fishery, Morton Reservoir, Mid Calder, W. Lothian. Tel: (0506) 882293.	Fly fishing only. Advance bookings. Double sessions May-Aug, 9 am-5 pm, 5 pm-dusk. Bag limits 3-6 fish per rod.
North Third	Cambusbarron	Rainbow/ Brown Trout		North Third Trout Fishery, "Greathill", Cambusbarron, Stirling. Tel: Stirling (0786) 71967.	Fly fishing only. Boat and bank. Brown and Rainbow Trout. Advance booking advisable.
Lochan Reoidhe	Aberfoyle	Brown Trout	15 Mar. to 6 Oct.	Forestry Commission David Marshall Lodge, Aberfoyle.	Fly fishing only. Limited rods. Boat available. Advance bookings accepted.
Threilpmuir Reservoir	Balerno	Brown/ Rainbow Trout	1 Apr. to 30 Sept.	Flemings, Grocer, Main Street, Balerno. Tel: 031-449 3833.	Limited number of permits covers Harlaw Reservoir as well.
Loch Venachar	Callander	Brown Trout	15 Mar. to 6 Oct.	J. Bayne, Main Street, Callander. Tel: (0877) 30218.	
Loch Voil	Balquhidder	Brown Trout Salmon	15 Mar. to 6 Oct.	Stronvar Country House Hotel, Balquhidder. Tel: (08774) 688.	Hotel Guests only. Advanced bookings necessary.
				C.M Oldham & I.T. Emslie, Muirlaggan, Balquhidder, Lochearnhead FK19 8PB. Tel: (08774) 219.	Boats. Two caravans to let with free fishing. Weekly bookings only.

FORTH AND LOMOND (CLYDE COAST)

Sea Angling
Helensburgh

Helensburgh is a small seaside town on the Firth of Clyde at the southern end of the Gareloch, easily reached by train or car.

Types of fish: Shore and boat – cod, flounder, coalfish, conger, rays, dogfish, whiting, dab, haddock, pollack and mackerel.

Bait: Ragworm, lugworm, may be dug locally. Mussels and crabs can be gathered from the shore.

Season for fishing: All year, especially winter for large cod.

Garelochhead

Garelochhead is the village at the head of the Gareloch, with the whole shoreline within easy reach. Upper and lower Loch Long and Loch Goil are only a few miles away.

Types of fish: Cod, coalfish, pollack, dab, flounder, plaice, whiting, haddock, pouting, rays, mackerel, spurdog, lesser spotted dogfish.

Bait: Garelochhead – cockles and mussels. Roseneath – lugworm, ragworm and cockles. Rhu – ragworm. Kilcreggan – ragworm. Coulport – cockles.

Season for fishing: December-March, migratory cod – June onwards.

Arrochar, Loch Long
The village lies at the northern end of the loch, and has waters sheltered by the high surrounding hills.

Types of fish: Shore – cod, conger, pollack, coalfish and rays. Boat – cod, haddock, whiting, conger, pollack, coalfish, mackerel, dogfish and rays.

Tackle: Available from Mr. Findlater, Braeside Stores, Arrochar.

Bait: Fresh herring and mackerel, mussels and cockles usually available from the pier. Artificial baits, lures etc. available from shops in village.

Season for fishing: All year.

Clynder
Clynder is the fishing centre on the sheltered west side of the Gareloch and one mile north of the popular Rhu Narrows.

Types of fish: Shore: cod and mackerel. Boat: cod, conger, rays, plaice, flounders, dogfish, whiting, pouting and mackerel.

Boats: C. Moar (0436) 831336;

Bait: Cockles, mussels, lug, ragworm, can be dug.

Season for fishing: All year, winter for large cod.

FORTH AND LOMOND (EAST COAST)
Anglers going afloat from Fife and Forth Harbours are advised to contact the coastguard at Fifeness for weather information. Tel: Crail (0333) 50666 (day or night).

Tayport
Tayport, on the Firth of Tay opposite Dundee, in the northern-most part of Fife, enjoys good shore fishing in sheltered waters. There are no hotels but there is a modern caravan and camping site with showers, laundry etc.

Types of fish: Cod, flounder and plaice from shore, with occasional sea trout (permit required).

Bait: Lugworm, ragworm, mussels, cockles and crabs available locally at low water.

Season for fishing: April- January.

St. Andrews
St. Andrews is a leading holiday resort with sea angling as one of its attractions. Fishing is mainly from boats, but good sport can be had from the rocks between the bathing pool and the harbour.

Tackle: Messrs. J. Wilson & Sons (Ironmongers), 169-171 South Street, St. Andrews, KY16 9EE, Tel: 0334 72477.

Bait: Excellent supplies of Lugworm, ragworm and large mussels can be gathered on the beach.

Boarhill and Kings Barns
Good beach fishing for cod and flatfish.

Anstruther
It is a fishing village with plenty of good boat and beach fishing. A very rocky coastline but can be very rewarding with good catches of cod, saithe, flounder, wrasse, and whiting. Be prepared to lose tackle.

Types of fish: Cod, saithe, wrasse, flounder, ling, conger and mackerel.

Boats: Plenty charter boats with local skippers who know all the hot spots.

Bait: Lug, rag, white rag, cockle, crab, mussel which can be dug locally.

Season: Boat – May-October. Beach – September-January.

Further information from: Mr. R. Paton, Buckhaven & District SAC, 46 West High Street, Buckhaven, KY8 1AL.

Pittenweem
The nerve centre of the East Neuk with a large deep water harbour which boats can enter or leave at any stage of the tide. The European Cod Festival is now held here each year and produces large catches of cod. The harbour wall is very popular with young and old alike, with some good catches.

Types of fish: Cod, saithe, flounder, wrasse, ling, conger, whiting, mackerel from boats. Cod, saithe, flounder, wrasse and whiting from beach.

Bait: Lug, rag, can be dug locally.

Season: Beach – September-January.

Leven
A holiday resort with about 2 miles of lovely sandy beaches. Beach fishing is very popular with some very good catches.

Types of fish: Flounder, cod, bass, mullet, saithe.

Boats: No charter boats.

Bait: Lug available locally.

Season: July-January.

Buckhaven
A small town on the north side of the Firth of Forth, which is renowned for its boat and beach fishing. The Scottish Open Beach Competition is fished from Buckhaven to Dysart each year with large entries from all over Scotland.

Types of fish: Cod, saithe, flounder, whiting, mackerel from beach. Cod, saithe, flounder, whiting, ling, mackerel and wrasse from boat.

Bait: Lug available at Leven.

Tackle: The Sports Shop, Wellesley Road, Buckhaven.

Boats: No charter hire.

Season: Boat – June-November. Beach – October-January.

Further information from: R. Paton, Buckhaven & District Sea Angling Club, 46 West High Street, Buckhaven KY8 1AL.

Kirkcaldy
Beach fishing at east and west end of town.

Types of fish: Cod, flatfish, saithe, mackerel.

Bait: Beach off bus station.

Pettycur and Kinghorn
Rock and beach fishing off Pettycur Harbour and Kinghorn Beach.

Types of fish: Saithe, flatfish.

Boats: Small boats can be launched from beaches.

Bait: Plenty locally. Local caravan sites.

Burntisland
Permission required to fish the beach from harbour to swimming pool.

Types of fish: Saithe, flatfish, small cod.

Boats: None locally.

Bait: Lug available locally.

South Queensferry
A picturesque burgh overshadowed by the Forth Bridges. There are 3 launching slips in the area, but currents can be dangerous and local advice should be obtained before setting out in dinghies.

Types of fish: Cod, whiting, coalfish, mackerel, flounder from boat and shore in season.

Bait: Lugworm, ragworm, mussel, cockle, clams and crabs at low water in the area.

Season for fishing: May to October.

Edinburgh
Scotland's capital city, on the south of the Forth estuary, has several miles of shoreline. Most of this is sandy, and can produce good catches of flatfish, although codling, Ray's bream, whiting, eels and mackerel can be taken in season from the shore. Best marks are at Cramond, round the mouth of the River Almond, and the Seafield to Portobello area.

Tackle: F. & D. Simpson, 28-29 West Preston Street, Tel: 031–667 3058 (permits available). Shooting Lines Ltd., 23 Roseburn Terrace, Tel: 031-337 8616.

Bait: Worms and maggots sold at Shooting Lines. Worms, maggots, shrimps and preserved sea baits sold at Simpsons. Lugworm, ragworm, mussels, cockles and clams from most beaches at low water.

Season for fishing: All year round.

Musselburgh
This town stands on the estuary of the River Esk, 6 miles to the east of Edinburgh, overlooking the Firth of Forth. It has a small but busy harbour at Fisherrow, catering mainly for pleasure craft.

Boats: Enquiries should be made at the harbour. Best shore marks range from Fisherrow harbour to the mouth of the Esk.

Bait: Lugworm, ragworm, mussels, cockles and clams at low water.

Further information from: Brunton Hall, East Lothian. Tel: 031-665 3711.

Cockenzie
Mullet can be caught around the warm water outfall to the east of Cockenzie Power station and around the harbour. Other species include flatfish, codling and mackerel.

North Berwick
There is good boat fishing out of North Berwick and the coastline between the town and Dunbar is good for shore fishing.

Types of fish: Cod, haddock, plaice, mackerel and coalfish.

Bait: Mussels, crabs and shellfish of various types available at low water.

Further information from: Information Centre, Quality Street. Tel: North Berwick (0620) 2197 January-December.

Dunbar
The coastline from Dunbar to Eyemouth is very popular for rock and beach fishing.

Types of fish: Cod, haddock, flounder, coalfish, mackerel, wrasse and whiting.

Boats: Details can be obtained from The Tourist Information Centre, Dunbar.

Tackle: Available from Dunbar and Messrs Main, Saddlers, West Port, Dunbar.

Bait: Mussels, lug and ragworm available at low water, and also from tackle dealers.

Season for fishing: Best April to October.

Further information from: Information Centre, Town House, High Street. Tel: Dunbar (0368) 63353 January-December.

Constituent Area Tourist Boards

City of Dundee Tourist Board
Director,
City of Dundee Tourist Board,
City Chambers,
Dundee DD1 3BY.
Tel: Dundee (0382) 23141.

Perthshire Tourist Board
Director of Tourism,
Perthshire Tourist Board,
The Round House,
Marshall Place,
Perth PH2 8NU.
Tel: Perth (0738) 27958.

Angus Tourist Board
Tourist Manager,
Angus Tourist Board,
Market Place,
Arbroath, Angus DD11 1HR.
Tel: Arbroath (0241) 72609/76680.

RIVER PURIFICATION BOARD
TAY RIVER PURIFICATION BOARD
3 South Street,
Perth, PH2 8NJ.
Tel: Perth 27989.

RIVERS

Water	Location	Species	Season	Permit available from	Other information
Braan	Amulree	Brown Trout	15 Mar. to 6 Oct.	Amulree Hotel, Amulree, by Dunkeld. Tel: (035 05) 218.	Private fishing for hotel residents only. Fly rods only.
Dean	Strathmore	Brown Trout	15 Mar. to 6 Oct.	Strathmore Angling Improvement Association, Mrs. A.J. Henderson, 364 Blackness Road, Dundee. Tel: (0382) 68062.	
Dochart	Killin	Brown Trout	15 Mar. to 6 Oct.	J. Lewis, Tackle Dealer, Killin, Perthshire. Tel: (056 72) 362.	All legal lures permitted. Fly only on lower beat.
Earn	Crieff	Salmon Sea Trout Brown Trout	1 Feb. to 30 Sep. 15 Mar.-15 Sept.	Crieff Angling Club. Mr. A. Boyd, King Street, Crieff. Tel: (0764) 3871.	No shrimp, prawn, diving minnow or floats. No bait before 1st May.
Ericht (and Ardle)	Bridge of Cally	Salmon Brown Trout	1 Jan.-15 Oct. 15 Mar. to 6 Oct.	Bridge of Cally Hotel, Blairgowrie, Perthshire. Tel: (025 086) 231.	Fly fishing only after 15 April.
	Craighall	Salmon Brown Trout	15 Jan.-15 Oct. 15 Mar to 6 Oct.	N.A. Rattray, Craighall-Rattray, Blairgowrie. Tel: (0250) 4749.	Subject to availability.
Isla	Strathmore	Brown Trout	15 Mar. to 6 Oct.	Strathmore Angling Improvement Association, Mrs. A.J. Henderson, 364 Blackness Road, Dundee. Tel: (0382) 68062.	
Lochay	Killin	Brown Trout Pike Perch	15 Mar. to 6 Oct.	J. Lewis, Tackle Dealers, Main Street, Killin, Perthshire. Tel: (056 72) 362.	Fly only on upper beat.

Water	Location	Species	Season	Permit available from	Other information
Lunan	Arbroath	Sea/ Brown Trout	15 Mar. to 6 Oct.	Arbroath Cycle and Tackle Centre, 274 High Street, Arbroath. Tel: (0241) 73467.	Fly, bait or spinning.
Lyon	Aberfeldy	Salmon	15 Jan. to 15 Oct.	Fortingall Hotel, Fortingall, by Aberfeldy. Tel: (088 73) 367.	No Sunday fishing.
	Tirinie Fishings	Salmon Brown Trout	15 Jan.-15 Oct. 15 Mar.-6 Oct.	Coshieville Hotel, By Aberfeldy PH15 2NE.	Max. 4 rods. No bait fishing. No Sunday fishing. Rods & ghillie available for hire.
South Esk	Kirriemuir	Salmon Sea Trout Brown Trout	16 Feb. to 31 Oct.	H. Burness, Kirriemuir Angling Club, 13 Clova Road, Kirriemuir. Tel: (0575) 73456. Permits issued only in advance.	No permits on Saturdays. No Sunday fishing. Fly only in parts in low water.
Tay	Aberfeldy	Brown Trout Grayling	15 Mar. to 6 Oct.	Jamiesons Sports Shop, 41 Dunkeld Street, Aberfeldy. Tel: (0887) 20385.	Fly only until 1st May.
		Salmon Brown Trout	15 Jan.-15 Oct. 15 Mar. to 6 Oct.	Weem Hotel, Aberfeldy. Tel: (0887) 20381.	
	Grandtully	Salmon Brown Trout Grayling	15 Jan.-15 Oct. 15 Mar. to 6 Oct.	Grandtully Hotel, Strathtay, Perthshire. Tel: (088 74) 207.	Fly, bait or spinning. Boat & ghillie available. Booking advisable.
	Dunkeld	Salmon Brown Trout	15 Jan.-15 Oct. 15 Mar.-6 Oct.	Stakis Hotels Ltd., Dunkeld House Hotel, Dunkeld. Tel: (03502) 771.	Two boats with two rods. Experienced ghillies. 8 bank rods. Tuition. No salmon fishing on Sundays. Booking advisable.
		Brown Trout	15 Mar. to 6 Oct.	Kettles of Dunkeld, Atholl Street, Dunkeld. Tel: (03502) 556.	Fly fishing only.
		Salmon Sea Trout Brown Trout	15 Jan.- 13 Oct. 12 Mar.- 6 Oct.	Tayside Hotel, Stanley, Nr. Perth. Tel: (0738) 828249.	Day permits available May-July. Hotel rates include fishing and holidays. Ghillies by arrangement. Advisable to book in advance.
	Perth	Salmon Sea Trout Flounders Roach	15 Jan. to 15 Oct.	Director of Leisure & Recreation, Perth & Kinross District Council, 3 High Street, Perth. Tel: (0738) 39911, (Monday to Friday). Tourist Information Centre, 45 High Street, Perth PH1 5TJ. Tel: (0738) 38353 Saturday.	Advisable to book in advance. Only 20 permits per day. Only 2 permits in advance by any one person. No weekly permits.
Tummel	Pitlochry	Salmon Sea Trout	15 Jan. to 15 Oct.	Pitlochry Angling Club c/o Tourist Office, Pitlochry. Tel: Mr. Gardiner (0796) 2157 (evenings).	Permits available Monday to Saturday.

Water	Location	Species	Season	Permit available from	Other information
Tummel contd.	Moulinearn to Ballinluig	Salmon Sea Trout	15 Jan. to 15 Oct.	Pitlochry Angling Club, c/o Tourist Office, Pitlochry. Tel: Mr. Gardiner, (0796) 2157 (evenings).	Only available July, August, September.
	Pitlochry to Ballinluig	Brown Trout Grayling	16 Mar. to 6 Oct.	Pitlochry Angling Club, Pitlochry Tourist Office. Ballinluig Post Office. Atholl Sports, Atholl Road, Pitlochry. Highland Gathering, 8 West Moulin Road, Pitlochry.	Five miles of river both banks. Map and rules on permit.

LOCHS AND RESERVOIRS

Water	Location	Species	Season	Permit available from	Other information
Butterstone Loch	Dunkeld	Rainbow/ Brown Trout	1 Apr. to 31 Oct.	The Bailiff, Lochend Cottage, Butterstone, by Dunkeld. Tel: (035 04) 238.	Fly fishing only. 12 Boats. Day Session: 9 am-5 pm. Evening: 5.30 pm-dusk.
Castlehill Reservoir	Glendevon	Brown Trout	1 Apr. to 30 Sept.	Craig Mitchell House. Or Boat House.	Fly fishing only.
Dunalastair Loch	Kinloch Rannoch	Brown Trout	15 Mar. to 6 Oct.	Lassintullich Fisheries. Tel: (08822) 238.	Five boats. No bank fishing. Fly fishing only.
Loch Earn	St. Fillans Lochearnhead	Brown Trout	15 Mar. to 6 Oct.	Post Office, St. Fillans. Post Office, Lochearnhead. D.A. Hotel, St. Fillans Clachan Hotel, Lochearnhead. Crumps Garage, Lochearnhead.	Fishing Mon. to Sun. Fly rod, Fly reel and any legal method, max. B.S. 4lbs. Min. taking size 8". Prohibited baits: diving minnow.
Loch Eigheach	Moor of Rannoch	Brown Trout	15 Mar. to 6 Oct.	Rannoch & District Angling Club, John Brown, The Square, Kinloch Rannoch. Tel: (088 22) 268.	Bank fishing only.
Loch Faskally	Pitlochry	Salmon	Mar., May to Oct.	E. Yule, Boathouse, Loch Faskally, Pitlochry. Tel: (0796) 2919/2938	Any legal lure for salmon
		Brown Trout Pike Perch	Apr. to Sept.		
Glendevon (Upper Reservoir Lower Reservoir)	Glendevon	Brown Trout	1 Apr. to 30 Sept.	Fife Regional Council, Craig Mitchell House. Flemington Road, Glenrothes.	Fly fishing only. No Sunday fishing. Bank fishing allowed on Lower Glendevon.
Heathery- ford	Just off Junction 6 on M90 at Kinross.	Brown/ Rainbow Trout	Mid-March to Dec.	Office on site, Tel: (0577) 64212.	All bank fishing, top quality trout. Trout master water.
Lochan- na-Laraig	Killin	Trout	15 Mar. to 6 Oct.	D. & S. Allan, Tackle Dealers, Main Street, Killin. Tel: (056 72) 362.	All legal lures.

Please mention this Pastime Publications Guide

Water	Location	Species	Season	Permit available from	Other information
Loch Leven	Kinross	Brown Trout (Loch Leven strain)	2nd Apr. to 6th Oct.	Lochleven Fisheries, The Pier, Kinross. Tel: Kinross 63407.	Fly and boat fishing only.
Lintrathen Reservoir	Kirriemuir	Brown Trout	1 Apr. to 6 Oct.	Lintrathen Angling Club Tayside Reg. Council, Water Services Dept., 10 Ward Road, Dundee. Tel: (0382) 21164. Club bookings: Dr. Parratt, 91 Strathearn Road, Broughty Ferry, Dundee. Tel: (0382) 77305. (Not after start of season).	Sixteen boats. Sunday fishing. Max. catch 24 fish per boat. Tel. for details of sessions.
Monzievaird	Crieff	Brown/ Rainbow Trout	Mar. to Oct.	J.D. Groot, Ochtertyre House, by Crieff, Perthshire. Tel: (0764) 3963.	Fly/boat fishing only. Sunday fishing. 9am-5pm (Mar.-Oct.). 5pm-dusk (June-Oct.)
Loch Rannoch	Kinloch Rannoch	Brown Trout	15 Mar. to 6 Oct.	Loch Rannoch Conservation Association, Cuilmore Cottage, Kinloch Rannoch. Loch Rannoch Hotel. Tel: (08822) 201. Bunrannoch Hotel,	Fly fishing only. 6 am - 10 pm. 15 foot open boats with outboards. No live bait. Ghillie service. Rod hire. Small tackle shop.
Rescobie Loch	Forfar	Brown/ Rainbow Trout	15 Mar. to 31 Oct.	Bailiff, Rescobie Loch. Tel: (030781) 384.	Fly fishing only. Bank & Boat.
Sandy-knowes Fishery	Bridge of Earn	Rainbow Trout	1 Mar. to 30 Nov.	M.A. Brien, The Fishery Office, Sandyknowe Fishery, Bridge of Earn. Tel: (0738) 813033.	Bank fly fishing only. Session times 10 am-2 pm, 2 pm-6 pm, 6 pm-10 pm. Bag limit - 4 trout per session. Open 7 days. No Sunday evenings.
Loch Tay	Killin	Trout	15 Mar. to 6 Oct.	D. & S. Allan, Tackle Dealers, Main Street, Killin. Tel: (056 72) 362. Claichaig Hotel, Killin. Tel: (056 72) 270.	All legal lures permitted.
	Milton Morenish	Salmon Trout	15 Jan.-15 Oct. 15 Mar.-6 Oct.	Loch Tay Highland Lodges, Milton Morenish, by Killin. Tel: (056 72) 323.	Sixteen boats available. Special offers for mid-week fishing.
	Ardeonaig	Salmon Trout Char	15 Jan.-15 Oct. 15 Mar. to 6 Oct.	Ardeonaig Hotel, South Loch Tay, by Killin. Tel: (056 72) 400.	Own harbour with 7 boats. both wooden and fibre glass, for trolling and drifting.
	Kenmore	Salmon Trout	15 Jan.-15 Oct. 15 Mar. to 6 Oct.	Kenmore Hotel, Kenmore, by Aberfeldy. Tel: (08873) 205.	Boats available on Loch Tay. Ghillie service, rod hire to residents. Fishing for two miles on River Tay.
Loch Turret	Crieff	Brown Trout	1 Apr. to 30 Sept.	Director of Finance, Central Scotland Water Board, 30 George Square, Glasgow. Tel: 041-248 5855. Mr. A. Boyd, King Street, Crieff. Tel: (0764) 3871.	Four boats with outboards. Fly only.

TAYSIDE
Sea Angling

Arbroath

Situated on the east coast of Angus, 17 miles north-east of Dundee, Arbroath is easily accessible by road and rail. It is the centre for commercial fishing, and famous for its smokies. Pleasure boats ply for short cruises to local sea cliffs and caves, from the harbour. There are about 10 boats between 15ft and 35ft used for lobster and crab fishing, taking out parties for sea angling.

Types of fish: Cod, coalfish, mackerel, flounder, conger, plaice, haddock and pollack.

Boats: Available through local fishermen and part time lobster and crab fishermen at reasonable prices.

Tackle: Available from Arbroath Cycle & Tackle Centre, 274 High Street, Arbroath DD11 1JE. Tel: Arbroath 73467.

Dundee

Dundee is situated on the estuary of the River Tay and has sea fishing in the city centre, while Broughty Ferry, a suburb of Dundee, Easthaven and Carnoustie, all within easy reach by road and rail, have sea fishing from rocks, piers or from boats. There are good marks around the Bell Rock about 12 miles offshore.

Types of fish: Cod, flatfish from shore plus cod, haddock, coalfish, ling, pouting and plaice from boats.

Tackle: available from Shotcast Ltd., 8 Whitehall Crescent, Dundee.

Bait: Available locally.

Season for fishing: All year.

Three codling at once for this lucky angler.

NORTHEAST and SPEY VALLEY RIVERS AND LOCHS

Constituent Area Tourist Organisations

Aviemore and Spey Valley Tourist Organisation
Area Tourist Officer,
Aviemore and Spey Valley Tourist Organisation,
Grampian Road, Aviemore,
Inverness-shire PH22 1PP.
Tel: Aviemore (0479) 810545.

Banff and Buchan Tourist Board
Tourism Manager,
Banff and Buchan Tourist Board,
Collie Lodge,
Banff AB4 1AU.
Tel: Banff (026 12) 2789.

Kincardine and Deeside Tourist Board
Tourist Officer,
Kincardine and Deeside Tourist Board,
45 Station Road, Banchory,
Kincardineshire AB3 3XX.
Tel: Banchory (033 02) 2066.

City of Aberdeen Tourist Board
Director,
City of Aberdeen Tourist Board,
St. Nicholas House, Broad Street,
Aberdeen AB9 1DE.
Tel: Aberdeen (0224) 632727.

Gordon District Tourist Board
Director,
Gordon District Tourist Board,
St. Nicholas House, Broad Street,
Aberdeen AB9 1DE.
Tel: Aberdeen (0224) 632727.

Moray District Council
Chief Tourist Officer,
Moray District Council,
17 High Street, Elgin,
Morayshire IV30 1EG.
Tel: Elgin (0343) 2666.

RIVER PURIFICATION BOARD
NORTH EAST RIVER PURIFICATION BOARD
Greyhope House,
Greyhope Road, Torry,
Aberdeen AB1 3RD.
Tel: Aberdeen (0224) 248338.

RIVERS

Water	Location	Species	Season	Permit available from	Other information
Avon	Ballindalloch	Salmon Sea Trout	11 Feb. to 30 Sept.	Delnashaugh Inn, Ballindalloch, Banffshire AB3 9AS. Tel: Ballindalloch 255.	No prawn. Fly fishing Sept. No lead attached to fly.
	Tomintoul	Salmon Sea Trout	Feb. to end Sept.	Gordon Arms Hotel, Tomintoul, Banffshire. Tel: Tomintoul 206.	No prawn. Fly fishing Sept. Max. breaking strain 10 lb. No lead attached to fly.
Bogie	Huntly	Salmon Sea Trout Brown Trout	11 Feb. to 31 Oct. 1 Apr. to 6 Oct.	Clerk of Fishings, Huntly Fishings Committee, P.O. Box 2, Royal Bank Buildings, 27/29 Duke Street, Huntly. Tel: (0466) 2291.	Permit covers Bogie, Deveron and Isla.
Carron	Stonehaven	Brown Trout	1 May to 31 Aug.	Davids Sports Shop, 31 Market Square, Stonehaven. Tel: Stonehaven 62239.	Visitors permits. Sea pool to railway viaduct.
Cowie	Stonehaven	Salmon Sea Trout Brown Trout	1 May to 31 Aug.	Davids Sports Shop, 31 Market Square, Stonehaven. Tel: Stonehaven 62239.	Visitors permits. Sea pool to railway viaduct.
Dee	Aboyne	Salmon Sea Trout Rainbow Trout	1 Feb. to 30 Sept.	Brooks House, Glen Tanar, Aboyne. Tel: (03398) 86451.	No Sunday fishing. Fly fishing only.

Water	Location	Species	Season	Permit available from	Other information
Dee contd.	Banchory	Salmon Sea Trout	1 Feb. to 30 Sept.	Banchory Lodge Hotel, Banchory. Tel: Banchory 2625.	Rods available by booking in advance.
	Blairs	Salmon Sea Trout	1 Feb. to 30 Sept.	Salar Properties UK Ltd., 60 Castle Street, Edinburgh EH2 3NA.	
Deveron	Huntly	Salmon Sea Trout Brown Trout	11 Feb. to 31 Oct. 1 Apr. to 6 Oct.	Clerk of Fishings, Huntly Fishings Committee, P.O. Box 2, Royal Bank Buildings, 27/29 Duke Street, Huntly. Tel: (0466) 2291.	Permits cover Deveron, Bogie and Isla.
		Salmon Sea Trout Brown Trout	Feb. to Oct.	Castle Hotel, Huntly. Tel: Huntly 2696.	
	Rothiemay	Salmon Sea Trout Brown Trout	11 Feb. to 31 Oct.	Forbes Arms Hotel, Rotheimay, Huntly. Tel: Rothiemay 248.	Fly fishing and spinning.
	Turriff	Salmon Sea Trout Brown Trout	11 Feb. to 31 Oct.	Turriff Ang. Assoc., I. Masson, The Cross, 6 Castle Street, Turriff. Tel: Turriff 62428.	No day tickets. Six weekly available to visitors. Restrictions on spinning.
Don	Glenkindie	Salmon Brown Trout	11 Feb.-31 Oct. 15 Mar.-1 Oct.	Glenkindie Arms Hotel, Glenkindie, by Alford. Tel: Glenkindie 41288.	May to Sept. fly only.
	Manar Fishings	Salmon Sea Trout Brown Trout	11 Feb. to 31 Oct. 1 Apr.-30 Sept.	J.J. Watson 44 Market Place, Inverurie. Tel: (0467) 20321.	No worm, shrimp or prawn. Limit of 8 rods per day.
	Kemnay	Salmon Brown Trout	11 Feb. to 31 Oct.	F.J. & S.L. Milton, Kemnay House, Kemnay, Aberdeenshire AB5 9LH. Tel: Kemnay 42220	Advance booking essential. Fly or spinning only.
	Strathdon	Salmon Brown Trout	11 Feb. to 31 Oct.	Colquhonnie Hotel, Strathdon, Aberdeenshire. Tel: (09756) 51210.	
	Kintore	Salmon Brown Trout	11 Feb. to 31 Oct.	Kintore Arms Inn, Kintore. Tel: Kintore 32216. J.A. Copland, Newsagent, 2 Northern Road, Kintore. Tel: Kintore 32210.	
	Inverurie	Salmon Sea Trout Brown Trout	11 Feb. to 31 Oct. 1 Apr.-30 Sept.	J.J. Watson, 44 Market Place, Inverurie. Tel: (0467) 20321.	No worm till 1 Apr. No natural minnow. No shrimp or prawn. Reductions for school children and OAP's.
Dulnain	Grantown-on-Spey	Salmon Sea Trout Brown Trout	11 Feb. to 30 Sept. 15 Mar.-30 Sept.	Strathspey Angling Assoc., Mortimer's, 61 High Street, Grantown-on-Spey. Tel: Grantown-on-Spey 2684.	Visitors resident in Grantown, Cromdale, Duthill, Carrbridge, Dulnain Bridge and Nethy Bridge areas. 12 miles of river.

Water	Location	Species	Season	Permit available from	Other information
Findhorn	Findhorn (Estuary)	Sea Trout	11 Feb. to 6 Oct.	Moray Water Sports, Findhorn.	Bait, fly, lures. Fly only 1 May-15 June.
	Forres	Salmon Sea Trout	11 Feb. to 30 Sept.	J. Mitchell, Tackle Shop, 97D High Street, Forres. Tel: Forres 72936.	Some private beats available.
Isla	Huntly	Salmon Sea Trout Brown Trout	11 Feb. to 31 Oct. 1 Apr. to 6 Oct.	Clerk of Fishings, Huntly Fishings Committee, P.O. Box 2, Royal Bank Buildings, 27/29 Duke Street, Huntly. Tel: (0466) 2291.	Permit covers Isla, Deveron and Bogie.
Muckle burn	Forres	Salmon Sea Trout	1 Apr. to 30 Sept.	J. Mitchell, Tackle Shop, 97D High Street, Forres. Tel: Forres 72923.	Reductions for juveniles
Spey	Aberlour	Salmon Sea Trout Brown Trout	11 Feb. to 30 Sept.	J.A.J. Munro, 93-95 High Street, Aberlour. Tel: Aberlour 428. Aberlour Hotel, Aberlour, Tel: Aberlour 287.	3 tickets per hotel, overnight accommodation in village hotel necessary prior to fishing. One fish above bridge (9 am-5 pm), one fish below bridge (9 am-midnight), other fish sold for club funds. No day tickets on Saturday or local holidays.
	Fochabers	Salmon	11 Feb. to 30 Sept.	Gordon Arms Hotel, Fochabers. Tel: (0343) 820508/9.	
	Grantown on-Spey	Salmon Sea Trout Brown Trout	11 Feb. to 30 Sept. 15 Mar.-30 Sept.	Strathspey Angling Assoc., Mortimer's 61 High Street, Grantown-on-Spey. Tel: Grantown-on-Spey 2684.	7 miles both banks. No prawn. No Sunday fishing. Visitors must reside in Grantown, Cromdale, Duthil, Carrbridge, Dulnain Bridge and Nethy Bridge.
	Boat of Garten	Salmon Sea Trout Brown Trout	11 Feb. to 30 Sept. 15 Mar.-30 Sept.	Craigard Hotel, Boat of Garten. Tel: Boat of Garten 206. The Boat Hotel, Boat of Garten. Tel: (047 983) 258. Allen's, Deshar Road, Boat of Garten. Tel: 372. River Spey	
	Nethy Bridge Boat of Garten	Salmon Sea Trout Brown Trout	11 Feb. to 30 Sept.	Abernethy Angling Assoc. Boat of Garten. Allen's, Deshar Road, Boat of Garten. Tel: 372.	
	Aviemore	Salmon Sea Trout Brown Trout	11 Feb. to 30 Sept.	Rothiemurchus Estate, Inverdruie, Aviemore. Tel: 810858. Kinrara Estate Office, Aviemore. Tel: (0479) 810207.	Four beats available on River Spey. Stocked rainbow trout loch.
	Aviemore	Salmon Sea Trout	11 Feb.-30 Sept. 15 Mar.-6 Oct.	Osprey Fishing School, The Fishing Centre, Aviemore. Tel: Aviemore 810911.	Fly fishing or spinning. River Spey, River Feshie and Lochs arranged.
		Rainbow Trout Brown Trout Salmon Sea Trout	11 Feb. to 30 Sept.	Alvie Estate Office, Kincraig, by Kingussie. Tel: Kincraig 255. Dalraddy Caravan Park, Aviemore. Tel: Aviemore 810330.	Fly fishing or spinning.

Water	Location	Species	Season	Permit available from	Other information
Ugie	Peter-head	Salmon Sea Trout Brown Trout	11 Feb. to 31 Oct.	Dicks Sports, 54 Broad Street, Fraserburgh. Robertson Sports, 1-3 Kirk Street, Peterhead AB4 6RT. Tel: (0779) 72584.	Bag limit - 8 fish per day. Fly, spinning or worm entire season. No shrimps, prawns or illegal baits.
Ury	Inverurie	Salmon Sea Trout Brown Trout	11 Feb. to 31 Oct. 1 Apr.-30 Sept.	J.J. Watson, 44 Market Place, Inverurie AB5 9XN. Tel: (0467) 20321.	No worm till 1 Apr. No natural minnow. No shrimp or prawn. Reductions for school children and OAP's.
Ythan	(Estuary) Newburgh	Salmon Sea Trout	11 Feb. to 31 Oct.	Mrs. Forbes, 3 Lea Cottages, Newburgh. Tel: (03586) 89297.	8 boats available. No lead core lines. No more than 2 lures or flies at one time. No live bait.
	Fyvie	Salmon Sea Trout	11 Feb. to 31 Oct.	Fyvie Angling Assoc., N. Rose, Clydesdale Bank plc, Fyvie, Turriff. Tel: (06516) 233.	

LOCHS AND RESERVOIRS

Water	Location	Species	Season	Permit available from	Other information
Aboyne Loch	Aboyne	Pike Perch		The Warden, Aboyne Loch, Holiday Park. Tel: Aboyne 86244.	Fishing parties restricted on Sat. and Sun. afternoons.
Loch Alvie	Aviemore	Brown Trout	15 Mar. to 6 Oct.	Kinrara Estate Office, Tel: (0479) 810207.	Three Boats.
		Brown Trout Pike		Alvie Estate Office, Kincraig, by Kingussie. Tel: Kincraig 255. Dalraddy Caravan Park, Aviemore. Tel: Aviemore 810330.	1 Boat. Fly fishing or spinning.
Avielochan	Aviemore	Rainbow/ Brown Trout	Apr. to Sept.	Mortimer's, 61 High St., Grantown-on-Spey. Tel: Grantown on Spey 2684.	Bank fishing only. Spinning area designated.
Loch of Blairs	Forres	Brown/ Rainbow Trout	Easter to Mid-Oct.	Moray District Council, Dept. of Recreation, 30-32 High Street, Elgin. Tel: Elgin 45121. J. Mitchell, 97D High St., Forres. Tel: Forres 72936.	Two sessions. Boat fishing. Fly only. Sunday fishing. 3 boats available.
Loch Dallas	Boat of Garten	Brown/ Rainbow Trout	Apr. to Sept.	Mortimer's 61 High Street, Grantown-on-Spey. Tel: Grantown on Spey 2684.	Fly fishing only.
Loch Ericht	Dalwhinnie	Brown Trout	15 Mar. to 6 Oct.	Badenoch Angling Association, Loch Ericht Hotel, Dalwhinnie.	

Water	Location	Species	Season	Permit available from	Other information
Glen Latterach Reservoir	Elgin	Brown Trout	1 Apr. to 30 Sept.	Moray District Council, Dept. of Recreation, 30-32 High Street, Elgin. Tel: Elgin 45121. Warden at Millbuies, Tel: (034 386) 234.	
Loch Insh	Kincraig	Salmon Sea Trout Brown Trout Char	11 Feb. to 30 Sept.	Alvie Estate Office, Kincraig, by Kingussie. Tel: Kincraig 255. Dalraddy Caravan Park, Aviemore. Tel: Aviemore 810330.	One boat. Boat fishing only. Fly fishing or spinning.
Millbuies Loch	Elgin	Brown/ Rainbow Trout	Easter to Mid-Oct.	Moray District Council, Dept. of Recreation, 30-32 High Street, Elgin. Tel: Elgin 45121. Warden at Millbuies. Tel: 034 386 234.	Boat fishing. Fly fishing only. Four boats available.
Loch Mor	Dulnain Bridge	Brown/ Rainbow Trout	Apr. to Sept.	Mortimer's 61 High Street, Grantown-on-Spey. Tel: (0479) 2684.	Fly fishing only.
Loch Na Bo	Lhanbryde	Brown Trout	1 Apr. to 30 Sept.	Keepers Cottage, Loch Na Bo. Tel: Lhanbryde 2214.	Fly fishing only.
Rothiemurchus Estate (Lochs, Fish farm, Pityoulish, Lily & Morlich)	Aviemore	Sea Trout Rainbow Trout Brown Trout Pike	Check with manager, Aviemore.	Rothiemurchus Fish Farm, Aviemore. Tel: Aviemore 810858.	
Loch Saugh	Fettercairn	Brown Trout	15 Mar. to 6 Oct.	Brechin Angling Club, W.G. Balfour, 9 Cookston Crescent, Brechin DD9 6BP. Tel: Brechin 2753. Ramsay Arms Hotel, Fettercairn. Tel: Fettercairn 334. Drumtochty Arms Hotel, Auchenblae AB3 1XR. Tel: (056 12) 210. David Rollston-Smith, 180 High Street, Montrose. Tel: (0674) 72692.	£3.50 per day.
Loch Vaa	Aviemore	Brown/ Rainbow Trout	Apr. to Sept.	Mortimer's 61 High Street, Grantown-on-Spey. Tel: Grantown-on-Spey 2684.	Boat fishing only.

FOLLOW THE COUNTRY CODE

NORTH EAST AND SPEY VALLEY

Sea Angling

Moray Firth
The Moray Firth has always been famous for its fishing grounds and most of the towns along the south coastline depend largely on commercial fishing for their prosperity; cod, haddock, flatfish of many kings, pollack, coalfish and mackerel being landed.

Nairn
Nairn is set on the pleasant coastal plain bordering the southern shore of the Moray Firth. There is a beautiful stretch of sands to the east. Most fishing is done from two small piers at the entrance to the tidal harbour.

Types of fish: Mackerel, small coalfish, pollack, dab and cod.

Boats: One or two, privately owned, will often take a passenger out. Enquiries should be made at the harbour.

Tackle: P. Fraser, 41 High Street, Nairn. Harbour Street General Store, Harbour Street.

Bait: Lugworm available on the beach at low water. Mackerel etc. mostly taken on flies.

Lossiemouth and Garmouth
Lossiemouth, a small, prosperous town, is a unique combination of white fish centre, seaside, shops and hotels. The angler will find unlimited sport of a kind probably new to him, for off the east and west beaches sea trout and finnock abound, and spinning for these into the sea, especially into the breakers, is a magnificent sport.

Types of fish: Sea trout, conger from the pier, coalfish, flatfish, 6½ miles of shore fishing. Haddock, cod, plaice and coalfish from boats. Shore fishing – sea trout between harbour and Boar's Head Rock and at the old cement works Garmouth.

Tackle: The Tackle Shop, 188 High Street, Elgin, Tel: 543129.

Bait: Lugworm on the west beach and the harbour at low water. Also plenty of mussels to be collected. Spinners, Pirks.

Permits: The Tackle Shop, 188 High Street, Elgin, Tel: 543129.

Season for fishing: Migratory fish season, October. Best months – late July, early August.

Buckie
Buckie is a major commercial fishing port on the eastern side of Spey Bay. It has become increasingly popular over the last few years as a tourist area and is well supplied with hotels, golf courses and caravan sites. It offers a varied coastline in the form of sandy beaches and quite spectacular rugged cliff formations.

Types of fish: Cod, coalfish, conger, pollack, mackerel, haddock, whiting, flatfish.

Tackle: Slater Sports, 2 Cluny Square, Buckie.

Bait: Lugworm, ragworm, mussels, cockles and crabs freely available along the shoreline eastwards.

Season for fishing: April-October. Winter months best for cod.

Portknockie
Portknockie is a quaint little fishing village to the west of Cullen Bay. The small harbour is used by two small mackerel boats.

Types of fish: Excellent rock fishing here for cod, coalfish, and some mackerel from the piers. Good boat fishing for haddock, ling and gurnard.

Boats: There are no boats for hire as such, although it is possible to get out in two small (18ft) mackerel boats.

Bait: Lugworm and mussels in the harbour at low water.

Further information from: Tourist Information Centre, 17 High Street, Elgin, IV30 1EG. Tel: (0343) 542666/543388.

Portsoy
One of the numerous small towns that line the Banffshire coast. It is a former seaport but the harbour is silting up.

Types of fish: Coalfish and mackerel from the small pier and some good rock fishing east and west for cod. From boats, mackerel, cod, haddock, plaice, coalfish and dab.

Bait: Some lugworm at low water mark.

Gardenstown and Crovie
These are traditional fishing villages. Mackerel are plentiful, June-September. Anglers would be well advised to follow local boats which are fishing commercially.

Types of fish: From shore – coalfish, pollack, flatfish, conger. From boats – mackerel, cod, haddock, flounder, plaice, conger, dab, catfish, gurnard and ling.

Bait: Available on beach, but local people prefer to use flies.

Fraserburgh
Situated on the north-east shoulder of Scotland, Fraserburgh has the Moray Firth to the west and north and the North Sea to the east. The Burgh was primarily given over to the herring and white fish industry, but has developed as a holiday resort with the decline of commercial fishing in the North Sea. Tickets and permits for game fishing from the beaches can be had at Weelies, Grocer, College Bounds.

Types of fish: Shore – cod, coalfish and mackerel. Boat – as shore.

Bait: Mussels and lugworm can be dug from the beach.

Season for fishing: May- October.

Peterhead
Peterhead is an important fishing port situated north of Buchan Ness, the most easterly point of Scotland. Excellent breakwaters, 1900ft and 2800ft long, are the main shore marks for holiday anglers. Access to the breakwaters is dependent on weather conditions and can be restricted when vessels are being worked. A safety access procedure has been agreed with the North Breakwater Sea Angling Society to whom further queries should be directed. However passengers are at times taken out by private boats.

Types of fish: From the pier – mackerel, coalfish, dab and cod. From boats – cod, haddock, dabs, ling, coalfish and mackerel.

Boats: There are a number of privately owned boats which will sometimes take out passengers. Enquiries should be made at the harbour.

Tackle: Available from Robertsons Sports, 1 Kirk Street, Peterhead.

Bait: Lugworm can be dug from shore at low water while mussels can be gathered from the rocks.

Stonehaven
Stonehaven is a holiday resort 15 miles south of Aberdeen on main road and rail routes. Magnificent catches of cod and haddock are taken regularly by boat. Anglers obtain great co-operation from angling boat skippers and local professional fishermen. On either side of Stonehaven there are good rock fishing marks which should be approached with care especially during strong easterly winds.

Types of fish: Cod, haddock, pollack, coalfish, flounder, catfish and mackerel from the shore. Cod, haddock, coalfish, pollack, ling, catfish, plaice and other flatfish, ballan wrasse, cuckoo wrasse, whiting and Norway haddock from boats.

Boats: Boats are available from skipper: A. McKenzie, 24 Westfield Park, Stonehaven, Tel: (0569) 63411 or Harbour Master, J. Lobban, Tel: (0569) 65323.

Bait: Mussels available if ordered from skippers of boats.

Season for fishing: All year.

Further information from: Information Centre, 66 Allardice Street, Tel: (0569) 62806 Easter-October.

GREAT GLEN and SKYE

RIVERS
AND LOCHS

Constituent Area Tourist Boards

Fort William and Lochaber Tourist Board
Area Tourist Officer,
Fort William and Lochaber Tourist Board,
Cameron Centre, Cameron Square,
Fort William,
Inverness-shire PH33 6AJ.
Tel: Fort William (0397) 3781.

Isle of Skye and South West Ross Tourist Board
Area Tourist Officer,
Isle of Skye and South West Ross Tourist Board,
Tourist Information Centre, Portree,
Isle of Skye IV51 9BZ.
Tel: Portree (0478) 2137.

Inverness, Loch Ness and Nairn Tourist Board
Area Tourist Officer,
Inverness, Loch Ness and Nairn Tourist Board,
23 Church Street,
Inverness IV1 1EZ.
Tel: Inverness (0463) 234353.

RIVER PURIFICATION BOARD
HIGHLAND RIVER PURIFICATION BOARD
Strathpeffer Road,
Dingwall IV15 9QY.
Tel: Dingwall 62021.

RIVERS

Water	Location	Species	Season	Permit available from	Other information
Coe	Glencoe	Salmon Sea Trout	15 Apr. to 15 Oct.	National Trust for Scotland, Achnambeithach Farm, Glencoe.	
Croe		Salmon Sea Trout	1 Mar. to 31 Oct.	National Trust for Scotland, Morvich Farm, Inverinate, By Kyle. Tel: Glenshiel (059981) 219.	
Enrick	Drumna-drochit	Salmon Brown Trout	15 Jan.-15 Oct. 15 Mar.-6 Oct.	Kilmartin Hall, Glenurquhart, Inverness-shire IV3 6TN. Tel: Glenurquhart 269.	
Garry	Invergarry	Salmon Brown Trout	15 Mar. to 6 Oct.	Garry Gualach, Invergarry. Tel: Tomdoun 230.	Fly only.
Lochy	Fort William	Salmon Sea Trout	May to Sept.	Rod & Gun Shop, Station Square, Fort William. Tel:(0397) 2656.	
Moriston	Glen-moriston Estuary beat Dundreggan	Salmon	15 Jan. to 15 Oct. Spring June onwards	Head Gamekeeper, A. Mackintosh, Tel: (0320) 51219.	
		Brown Trout	Mar. to Sept.		
Nairn	Nairn	Salmon Sea Trout	11 Feb.-30 Sept.	Nairn Angling Association P. Fraser, High Street, Nairn. Clava Lodge Holiday Homes, Culloden Moor, Inverness. Tel: Culloden Moor (0463) 790228, Inverness (0463) 790405.	

126

Water	Location	Species	Season	Permit available from	Other information
Nevis	Fort William	Salmon Sea Trout		Rod & Gun Shop Station Square, Fort William. Tel: (0397) 2656.	
Ose	Skye	Salmon Sea Trout	11 Feb. to 31 Oct.	Ullinish Lodge Hotel, Struan, Isle of Skye. Tel: (047 072) 214.	Residents only.
Snizort	Skye	Salmon Sea Trout Brown Trout	1 Jul. to 31 Oct.	Skeabost House Hotel, Skeabost, Isle of Skye. Tel: Skeabost Bridge 202.	Discounts for residents.
		Salmon Sea Trout Brown Trout	11 Feb. to 31 Oct.	Ullinish Lodge Hotel, Struan, Isle of Skye. Tel: (047072) 214.	Residents only.

LOCHS

Water	Location	Species	Season	Permit available from	Other information
Ardtornish Estate Waters	Morvern	Salmon Sea Trout Brown Trout	Apr.-Oct.	Ardtornish Estate Office, Morvern, by Oban, Argyll. Tel: (096 784) 288.	Six boats for hire.
Loch Arkaig	Fort William	Sea Trout Brown Trout Salmon (occasional) Pike	Mar.-Oct.	Locheil Estate Fishings, West Highland Estates Office, 33 High Street, Fort William. Tel: Fort William 2433. Tel: Spean Bridge 783.	
Loch Benevean (Bheinn a' Mheadhoin)	Cannich	Brown Trout	15 Mar. to 6 Oct.	J. Graham & Co., 71 Castle Street, Inverness. Tel: (0463) 233178.	Fly fishing only.
Lochs Connan (Duagraich & Ravag)	Skye	Brown Trout	15 Mar. to 6 Oct.	Ullinish Lodge Hotel, Struan, Isle of Skye. Tel: (047 072) 214.	Sunday fishing permitted.
Loch Dochfour	Inverness	Brown Trout	15 Mar. to 6 Oct.	Dochfour Estate Office, Dochgarroch, by Inverness. Tel: Dochgarroch 218.	No Sunday fishing. Bank fishing only.
Loch Garry (and Loch Inchlaggan)	Invergarry	Brown Trout Arctic Char	May-Sept.	Garry Gualach, Invergarry, Inverness-shire. Tel: Tomdoun 230.	Boats available. Loch Inchlaggan fly only.
Loch Morar (and hill lochs)	Morar	Salmon Sea Trout Brown Trout	11 Feb. to 1 Nov. 15 Mar. to 6 Oct.	Morar Hotel, Morar.	For guests only. Three boats available.
Loch Ness	Foyers	Salmon Brown Trout	15 Jan. to Oct.	The Foyers Hotel, Foyers, Inverness-shire. Tel: Gorthleck 216.	
Loch Ruthven	Farr	Brown Trout	15 Mar. to 6 Oct.	J. Graham & Co., 71 Castle Street, Inverness. Tel: Inverness 233178.	Fly fishing only.

Water	Location	Species	Season	Permit available from	Other information
Loch Ruthven contd.	Glenfinnan	Salmon Sea Trout	Apr.-Oct.	The Stage House, Glenfinnan, Inverness-shire. Tel: (039 783) 246.	Six boats available with outboards.
				Glenfinnan House Hotel, Glenfinnan. Tel: (039 783) 235.	Three boats available.
South Skye Fishings	South Skye	Sea Trout Brown Trout	Apr.-Oct.	Fearann Eilean Iarmain, Eilean Iarmain, An t-Eilean, Sgitheanach, Tel: (047 13) 266. Telex: 75252 iarman g.	
Storr Lochs (and other hill lochs)	North Skye	Brown Trout	15 Mar. to 30 Sept.	Anderson, MacArthur & Co., Somerled Square, Portree. Tel: (0478) 2197.	
Whitebridge Lochs (Knockie & Bran)	White-bridge	Brown Trout	Mar.-Oct.	Whitebridge Hotel, Stratherrick, Gorthleck, Inverness-shire. Tel: Gorthleck 226.	Boats available. Fly fishing only.

GREAT GLEN AND ISLE OF SKYE

Sea Angling

Isle of Eigg

The Isle of Eigg lies 5m SW of Skye.

Types of fish: Pollack, conger, spurdog, skate, cod, mackerel.

Season for fishing: Summer-Autumn.

Isle of Skye

The many lochs and bays around the beautiful Isle of Skye provide ideal facilities for sea angling. There is a great variety of fish, most of which can be caught from the shore because of the deep water found close inshore off rocky shores and headlands. Local residents are very knowledgeable about fishing in their own area. Loch Snizort has now been found to hold a number of large common skate and anglers could well contact these during a session there.

Isle of Skye (Portree)

Portree, the capital of Skye, is situated half way up the east coast of the island. There is a very good harbour and good fishing marks in and round it. Ample free anchorage and berthing available for visiting craft. Slipping, re-fuelling and watering facilities are easily accessible.

Types of fish: Cod, haddock, whiting, coalfish, pollack and mackerel.

Boats: Greshornish House Hotel, Edinbane, by Portree. Tel: (047082) 266, has one boat available.

Bait: Unlimited mussels and cockles available in tidal area of Portree Bay.

Tackle: North Skye Fishermen, Quay Street, Portree.

Season for fishing: May-September.

Further information from: Isle of Skye & South West Ross Tourist Board, Tourist Information Centre, Portree (0478) 2137.

Isle of Skye (Camastianavaig by Portree)

To reach this sheltered bay which lies 4 miles south east of Portree, turn off the A850 to Braes. Although local tactics are the use of feathers, bottom fishing with trace or paternoster has yielded heavy bags with skate of 62½lbs, cod 6lbs, whiting 3lbs, haddock 3lbs, spurdog 12lbs, gurnard 2lbs, pollacks 12lbs, coalfish 14lbs, all from boats.

Types of fish: Shore – coalfish, pollack, wrasse and mackerel. Boat – cod, haddock and spurdog.

Tackle: Obtainable at Portree.

Bait: Lugworm at Broadford Bay and Balmeanac Bay. Cockles and mussels at Portree Loch.

Season for fishing: June- October.

Isle of Skye (Uig)

Uig, a picturesque village amidst some of the finest scenery in the north west, has excellent fishing on its doorstep. Loch Snizort and small islands at its entrance, together with the Ascrib Islands opposite, are well worth fishing. Fishing can be arranged as far round the coast as Score Bay, known to some ring net fishermen as the 'Golden Mile'.

Types of fish: Shore – coalfish, mackerel, pollack, conger and dogfish. Boat – coalfish, mackerel, pollack, conger, whiting, haddock, dogfish, flatfish, skate, cod and gurnard.

Boats: Available locally at Uig, Waternish and Kilmuir.

Season for fishing: May-September.

Isle of Skye (Skeabost Bridge)

Skeabost Bridge is situated 5 miles from Portree at the south east end of Loch Snizort.

Types of fish: There is no shore fishing but many types of sea fish can be caught from boats.

Bait: Available locally.

Season for fishing: July- October.

Kyle of Lochalsh

The village of Kyle, on the mainland opposite Kyleakin on the Isle of Skye, is a railhead and a car ferry link with Skye and the Hebrides.

Types of fish: Conger, coalfish, pollack and whiting from the harbour. Boat – pollack, cod, coalfish, mackerel and whiting.

Tackle: Available from Marine Stores, Kyle of Lochalsh. IV40 8AE. Tel: (0599) 4208.

Bait: Mussels from Fishery Pier and clams and cockles at spring tides.

Season for fishing: June-September.

Further information from: Isle of Skye & South West Ross Tourist Board, Tourist Information Centre, Kyle of Lochalsh. Tel: (0599) 4276.

Constituent Area Tourist Boards

Caithness Tourist Board
Area Tourist Officer,
Caithness Tourist Board,
Whitechapel Road, Wick,
Caithness KW1 4EA.
Tel: Wick (0955) 2596.

Sutherland Tourist Board
Area Tourist Officer,
Sutherland Tourist Board,
The Square, Dornoch,
Sutherland IV25 3SD.
Tel: Dornoch (0862) 810400

Ross and Cromarty Tourist Board
Area Tourist Officer,
Ross and Cromarty Tourist Board,
Information Centre, North Kessock,
Inverness IV1 1XB.
Tel: Kessock (0463 73) 505.

RIVER PURIFICATION BOARD
HIGHLAND RIVER PURIFICATION BOARD
Strathpeffer Road,
Dingwall IV15 9QY.
Tel: Dingwall 62021.

RIVERS

Water	Location	Species	Season	Permit available from	Other information
Alness	Alness	Salmon Sea Trout	11 Feb. to 15 Oct.	Coul House Hotel, Contin by Strathpeffer IV14 9EY. Tel: (0997) 21487.	Six beats available on rotation. Four rods per beat. Fly fishing only.
Conon	Contin	Salmon Sea Trout	26 Jan. to 30 Sept.	Coul House Hotel, Contin, by Strathpeffer, Ross-shire. Tel: Strathpeffer 21487.	Lower/middle/upper Brahan. Coul water & lower Fairburn beats various times. Ghillies, boats. Fly (& spinning until end May).
Lower Conon	Dingwall	Salmon Sea Trout	26 Jan. to 30 Sept.	Dingwall & District Angling Club, c/o Sports & Model Shop, Tulloch Street, Dingwall. Tel: (0349) 62346.	Fly only. Breast waders prohibited.
		Brown Trout		Seaforth Highland Estate, Brahan, Dingwall. Tel: (0349) 61150.	
Dionard	Durness	Salmon Sea Trout		Cape Wrath Hotel, Durness.	
Halladale	Forsinard (2 mile upper beat)	Salmon	11 Jan. to 30 Sept.	Forsinard Hotel, Forsinard, KW13 6YT. Tel: (06417) 221.	Fly fishing only (spate river).
	Forsinard to Melvich Bay	Salmon	Jan. to 30 Sept.	Mrs. J. Atkinson, 8 Sinclair Street, Thurso, Caithness.	Trout fishing on lochs also available.
Helmsdale	Helmsdale	Salmon Sea Trout	11 Jan. to 30 Sept.	Strathullie Crafts, Dunrobin Street, Helmsdale KW8 6AH. Tel: (043 12) 343.	Assocation beat. Fly only.
Kerry	Gairloch	Salmon Sea Trout		Creag Mor Hotel, Charleston, Gairloch, Ross-shire. Tel: (0445) 2068.	

Water	Location	Species	Season	Permit available from	Other information
Kirkaig	Lochinver	Salmon	1 May to 15 Oct.	Inver Lodge Hotel, Lochinver IV27 4LU. Tel: (05714) 496.	
Oykel	Sutherland	Salmon Sea Trout	11 Jan. to 30 Sept.	Inver Lodge Hotel, Lochinver IV27 4LU. Tel: (05714) 496.	
Thurso	Thurso/ Halkirk	Salmon	11 Jan. to 5 Oct.	Thurso Fisheries Ltd., Thurso East, Thurso. Tel: (0847) 63134.	Fly fishing only.
Torridon	Torridon	Salmon Sea Trout	1 May to 31 Oct.	Loch Torridon Hotel, Torridon, by Achnasheen, Ross-shire. Tel: (044 587) 242.	Fly fishing angling instruction.
Ullapool	Ullapool	Salmon Sea Trout Brown Trout	May to 30 Sept.	Loch Broom Hardware Shop, Ullapool. Tel: (0854) 2356.	
Wick	Wick	Salmon Brown/ Sea Trout	11 Feb. to 21 Oct.	Hugo Ross, Tackle Shop, 16 Breadalbane Cres. Wick. Tel: (0955) 4200.	Fly/worm fishing. Spate River with good holding pool.

LOCHS

Water	Location	Species	Season	Permit available from	Other information
Loch Achall	Ullapool	Salmon Sea Trout Brown Trout	1 April to 30 Sept.	Loch Broom Hardware Shop, Ullapool. Tel: (0854) 2356.	Boat and bank fishing.
Loch A'chroisg	Achnasheen	Pike Perch		Ledgowan Lodge Hotel, Achnasheen, Ross-shire. Tel: Achnasheen 252.	Free to residents.
Loch a'Ghriama	Nr. Lairg	Brown Trout Occasional Salmon	30 Apr. to 30 Sept.	Overscaig Lochside Hotel, Loch Shin, By Lairg IV27 4NY. Tel: 054 983 203.	Boats available. Fly only. No Sunday fishing.
Loch Assynt (and Lochs Awe, Gillaroo, Grugach Borralam Cam Letteressie Loch)	Inchnadamph	Salmon Brown Trout	1 Apr.-15 Oct. 1 Apr.-6 Oct.	Inchnadamph Hotel, Assynt, by Lairg IV27 4HL. Tel: (05712) 202.	No Sunday fishing. Boats available.
Loch Badanloch (and other hill lochs)	Kinbrace	Brown Trout	15 Mar. to 6 Oct.	Richard McNicol, Badanloch, Kinbrace, Sutherland. Tel: Kinbrace 232.	Nine boats. Fly only.
Loch Borralie	Durness	Brown Trout		Cape Wrath Hotel, Keoldale, by Lairg, Sutherland. Tel: (097181) 274.	Limestone loch. Fly fishing only. Boats available.
Loch Brora	Brora	Salmon Sea Trout Trout	Apr. to Oct.	Rob Wilson, Fountain Square, Brora, Sutherland. Tel: Brora 21373.	Boats - Rob Wilson & Royal Marine Hotel Tel: (0408) 21252,

Water	Location	Species	Season	Permit available from	Other information
Loch Caladail	Durness	Brown Trout		Cape Wrath Hotel, Keoldale, by Lairg, Sutherland. Tel: (097181) 274.	Limestone loch. Fly fishing only. Boats available.
Loch Calder	Thurso	Brown Trout	15 Mar. to 6 Oct.	None required	All legal methods.
Cape Wrath hill lochs (30 plus)	Durness	Brown Trout		Cape Wrath Hotel, Keoldale, by Lairg, Sutherland. Tel: (097181) 274.	
Loch Craggie	Tongue	Brown/ sea/ Rainbow Trout	15 Mar. to 6 Oct.	Tongue Hotel, Tongue. Tel: Tongue 206. Ben Loyal Hotel, Tongue. Tel: Tongue 216. Post Office, Tongue. Royal Bank, Tongue.	Fly fishing only. Boat available.
Loch Croispol	Durness	Brown Trout		Cape Wrath Hotel, Keoldale, by Lairg, Sutherland. Tel: (097181) 274.	Limestone loch. Fly fishing only. Boats available.
Loch Culag (Fionn Loch and numerous others)	Lochinver	Brown/ Rainbow Trout	15 Mar. to 6 Oct.	Inver Lodge Hotel, Lochinver, Sutherland. Tel: Lochinver 496.	
Dornoch & District Angling Assoc. (7 lochs)	Dornoch	Brown Trout Sea Trout Salmon	15 Mar. to 6 Oct.	Dornoch & District Angling Association, William A. McDonald, Castle Street, Dornoch. Tel: Dornoch 810301.	No Sunday fishing. Fly fishing only. 7 boats available.
Dunnet-Head Lochs	Dunnet-Head (B855)	Brown Trout	May to Oct.	Dunnet Head Tearoom, Brough Village, Dunnet Head. Tel: 084-785-774.	Lochs well stocked. Fly from bank only. No Sunday fishing. £2 day, £5 week. Sea fishing from rocks.
Fionn Loch	Gairloch	Salmon Brown Trout		H. Davis, Creag Beag, Gairloch. Tel: (0445) 2322.	Fly only.
Forsinard Lochs (Loch Sletill and many others)	Forsinard	Brown Trout	1 May. to 30 Sept.	Forsinard Hotel, Forsinard, Sutherland. Tel: Halladale 221.	Fly fishing only. 5 Boats. Bank and boat fishing.
	Kyle of Tongue	Sea Trout Salmon	11 Feb. to 31 Oct.	Tongue Hotel, Tongue. Tel: Tongue 206. Ben Loyal Hotel, Tongue. Tel: Tongue 216. Post Office, Tongue. Royal Bank, Tongue.	No Sunday fishing. Bank only.
Golspie Angling Club waters (Loch Brora Loch Lundie Loch Horn)		Salmon Sea Trout Brown Trout	15 Mar. to 15 Oct.	Golspie Angling Club, Lindsay & Co., Main Street, Golspie. Tel: (04083) 212.	Fly fishing only. Bank and boat fishing. No Sunday fishing.

Water	Location	Species	Season	Permit available from	Other information
Loch Hope	10 miles West of Tongue	Sea Trout Salmon	18 June to 30 Sept.	Ian MacDonald, The Keepers House, Hope, by Lairg. Tel: 084 756 272.	Fly fishing from boats only. Two rods per boat.
Loch Kernsary (Tournaig Goose Ghiuragarstidh)	Gairloch	Brown Trout	15 Mar. to 6 Oct.	National Trust for Scotland, Inverewe Visitor Centre, Poolewe, Ross-shire. Tel: (044586) 229.	
Leckmelm Hill Lochs	Ullapool	Brown Trout	May to Sept.	Leckmelm Holiday Cottages, Leckmelm, Ullapool. Tel: (0854) 2471.	Bank fishing only. No Sunday fishing.
Loyal	Tongue	Brown Trout Sea Trout Salmon	15 Mar.-6 Oct.	Tongue Hotel, Tongue. Tel: Tongue 206. Ben Loyal Hotel, Tongue. Tel: Tongue 216. Post Office, Tongue. Royal Bank, Tongue.	Fly fishing only. Bank only.
Loch Maree	Ross-shire	Salmon Sea Trout Brown Trout	May-Oct.	Loch Maree Hotel, Achnasheen. Tel: Kinlochewe 288.	Several Boats
				Kinlochewe Hotel, Kinlochewe. Tel: Kinlochewe 253.	Two boats.
Melvich hill lochs	Melvich	Brown Trout	Jun-Sept.	Melvich Hotel, Melvich, by Thurso, KW14 7YS. Tel: (06413) 206.	
Loch Merkland	Nr. Lairg	Brown Trout Occasional Salmon	30 Apr. to 30 Sept.	Overscaig Lochside Hotel, Loch Shin, by Lairg IV27 4NY. Tel: 054 983 203.	Boat available. Fly only. No Sunday fishing.
Loch Morie	Head of River Alness	Brown Trout Arctic Char	15 Mar. to 6 Oct.	Coul House Hotel, Contin, by Strathpeffer, Ross-shire. Tel: Strathpeffer 21487.	Boat available.
Scourie Lochs (over 200 available)	Scourie	Salmon Sea Trout Brown Trout	1 Jul.-15 Oct. 1 May-30 Sept.	Scourie Hotel, Scourie, by Lairg, Sutherland. Tel: Scourie 2396.	Twelve boats available. No Sunday fishing. Fly fishing only.
Loch Shin	Overscaig by Lairg	Brown Trout 'Ferox' Trout Occasional Salmon	30 Apr. to 30 Sept.	Overscaig Lochside Hotel, Loch Shin, by Lairg IV27 4NY. Tel: 054 983 203	Boats and outboards available.
Loch Sionascaig (and other lochs)	Ullapool	Brown Trout		Inverpolly Estate Office, Inverpolly, Ullapool. Tel: Achiltibuie 452.	
Slaim	Tongue	Brown Trout Salmon Sea/ Rainbow Trout		Tongue Hotel, Tongue. Tel: Tongue 206.	Fly fishing. Boats available.

Water	Location	Species	Season	Permit available from	Other information
Tarvie Trout Lochs	By Contin	Stocked Brown/ Rainbow Trout		Sports & Model Shop, Tulloch Street, Dingwall. Tel: (0349) 62346.	Fly only, Boat fishing. "Troutmaster water".
Tongue Lochs (14)	Tongue	Brown Trout	15 Mar. to 6 Oct.	Tongue Hotel, Tongue. Tel: Tongue 206. Bcn Loyal Hotel, Tongue. Tel: Tongue 216. Post Office, Tongue. Royal Bank, Tongue.	
Ulbster Estates Lochs (9 hill lochs)	Halkirk	Brown Trout	15 Mar. to 6 Oct.	Ulbster Arms Hotel, Halkirk, Caithness. Tel: Halkirk 206.	No Sunday fishing. Fly fishing only. One boat on each of five lochs.
Loch Watten	Watten Village	Brown Trout	1 May to 30 Sept.	Hugo Ross, Tackle Shop, 16 Breadalbane Cres. Wick. Tel: (0955) 4200.	Boats for hire from tackle shop. Fish min. size 10". No Sunday fishing.

NORTH SCOTLAND
Sea Angling

Gairloch
Gairloch Bay is very popular with sea anglers. There is good fishing in this lovely sea loch, especially around Longa Island which lies near the entrance to the Loch.

Poolewe and Aultbea
Situated amidst magnificent scenery, the sheltered waters of Loch Ewe offer the sea angler opportunities of fine catches. Suitable accommodation is available in surrounding villages and local advice is always available.

Types of fish: Shore – pollack, coalfish, dab, codling. Boat – haddock, cod, codling, gurnard, skate, whiting, mackerel, flatfish.

Boats: Several boats available locally.

Bait: Mussels, lugworm, cockles, etc. from shore. Artificial and preserved baits from D. Toop, Bridgend Stores, Aultbea, Tel: Aultbea 204.

Season for fishing: April- October incl.

Little Loch Broom
Ten miles north east Aultbea.
Ullapool & The Summer Isles
Loch Broom and the waters encircled by the Summer Isles offer excellent sea angling. The banks can be approached from Ullapool, which is an attractive holiday village sited on a peninsula projecting into Loch Broom. The numerous banks and islands offer superb fishing and beautiful scenery in sheltered waters. Many attractions on shore via local shops; hotels and sporting facilities available throughout the season. Morefield Motel, Ullapool. Tel: Ullapool (0854) 2161 offers day charters. Achiltibuie, a small village, also gives access to fishing grounds.

Types of fish: Shore – codling, coalfish, conger, pollack, mackerel, dabs, thornbacks, dogfish, flounders and plaice. Boat – as above plus haddock, whiting, wrasse, ling, megrim, gurnard, spurdog and turbot.

Tackle: Lochbroom Hardwear. Ullasport.

Season for fishing: June- October inclusive. Big skate best in autumn.

Lochinver
Lochinver is one of the major fishing ports in the north of Scotland. With a population of some 300 inhabitants it has a safe all - tides harbour with excellent shore services, including good moderately - priced accommodation and two fishing tackle shops. Excellent sea fishing within a short distance from the port, specialising in jumbo haddock, cod, skate and conger. It is one of the few areas where large halibut are caught. Boats available. A large fleet of fishing vessels operates from the harbour and bait is readily available.

Types of fish: Cod, haddock, whiting, saithe, gurnard, ling, pollack, mackerel, wrasse, conger, skate. Coalfish, pollack, cod and mackerel from the shore.

Tackle: Tackle is available from Lochinver Fish Selling Co.
Season for fishing: April- October.
Drumbeg
Seven miles north of Lochinver.
Caithness
With the prolific fishing grounds of the Pentland Firth, the north of Caithness has built up a reputation as being one of the premier sea angling areas in Scotland. It is now recognised that the chance of taking a halibut on rod and line is better in Pentland waters than anywhere else; more halibut have been taken here than in any other part of the British Isles. The presence of Porbeagle shark in these waters has been proved by the capture of two specimens, with many more hooked and lost. Among the notable fish caught were European halibut records of 194 lbs. in 1974, 215 lbs. in 1975, 224 lbs. in 1978 and 234 lbs. in 1979. This fish represented a world record catch for the species. The Scottish shore record ling of 12lbs 4oz was caught in these waters. With countless numbers of rocky coves and sandy beaches there is much for the shore angler to discover along the whole of the north coast of Scotland. Accommodation is available to suit everyone, from first class hotels, private B. & B. to caravan and camping sites with full facilities. It is also possible to have a full sea angling package holiday with full board at a hotel and all boat charges included. The number of angling boats available increases each year, but it is still advisable to book boat places in advance.

Thurso and Scrabster

Thurso is the main town on the north side of Caithness and gives access through Scrabster to the waters of the Pentland Firth, where there are first class fishing grounds. Thurso Bay and the Dunnet Head area are sheltered from prevailing winds and it is reasonably easy for anglers to get afloat to the marks. Scrabster 1¼ miles from Thurso, is the main harbour in northern Caithness. Most of the angling boats are based here. There is also some excellent rock fishing, while conger may be caught from the harbour walls.

Types of fish: Cod, ling, haddock, conger, pollack, coalfish, dogfish, spurdog, plaice, wrasse, mackerel, dab, whiting, rays, halibut, porbeagle shark.

Boats: Mr. F. Johnson, 110 High Ormlie, Thurso. Tel: (0847) 63313/65406.

Tackle: Harper's Fly Fishing Services, The Drill Hall, Sinclair Street, Thurso.
C.H. Haygarth & Sons, Gunmakers & Fishing Tackle, The Cottage Gun Shop, Dunnet, Caithness KW14 8XQ, Tel: 0847 85602 (adj. to St. John's Loch).

Bait: Mussels, lugworm can be gathered at low water, mackerel and squid from fish shops and local fishermen. Most species take lures, feather and rubber eels, etc. and most fishing done with this type of artificial bait.

Season for fishing: April-November.

Further information from: Mr. Holmes, Flat 15, Braal Castle, Halkirk, Caithness or Caithness Tourist Board, Whitechapel Road, Wick, Tel: (0955) 2596 Jan-Dec.

Dunnet

Dunnet is situated 8 miles east of Thurso at the end of the famous Dunnet Sands, which are over 2½ miles long. Few anglers fish this beach, as there is excellent boat fishing nearby. There is plenty of lugworm and the beach is well worth trying.

Types of fish: As for Thurso.

Boats and Tackle: As for Thurso.

Bait: Mussels from the rocks at low tide and lugworm all along Dunnet Sands.

Season for fishing: Shore – July and August. Boat – April-November.

Keiss

Good shore fishing is to be had around Keiss, a small fishing village between John o'Groats and Wick. It might be difficult to get out in a boat. The shore fishing is from the rocks around Keiss, and from the beach at Sinclair's Bay to the south of the village. Here some very good plaice have been taken and also anglers have caught sea trout while spinning for mackerel.

Tackle: Tackle shops at Wick.

Bait: Mussels and lugworm can be obtained at low tide.

Sutherland and Easter Ross Brora

Brora is a village situated on the A9, 12 miles south of Helmsdale. There is a small harbour and a few boats are available to sea anglers. There are rail links to Brora from the south and ample hotel accommodation and caravan facilities.

Types of fish: Cod, coalfish, cod, ling, haddock, rays and conger from boats.

Boats: Some owners are willing to take visitors at nominal costs.

Tackle: Rob Wilson, Fountain Square, Brora.

Bait: Can be dug locally.
Season for fishing: July-September.

Grannies Heilan' Hame, Embo

This is a caravan holiday centre with extensive amenities 2 miles north of Dornoch.

Types of fish: Spinning for sea trout from the beach up to the mouth of Loch Fleet. Coalfish, mackerel and flatfish from the pier. The rocks provide good cod fishing. From boats, coalfish, mackerel, plaice, cod, haddock and whiting at times.

Bait: Lugworm can be dug at the ferry landing area and there are plenty of mussels and cockles near Loch Fleet.

Season for fishing: April-September.

Dornoch

Dornoch gives access to the fishing banks off the north coast of the Dornoch Firth. There is good shore fishing from the rocks at Embo, but to get afloat it is necessary to make arrangements in advance. Youngsters can enjoy good fishing from Embo Pier.

Types of fish: Sea trout from shore. Flat fish, haddock and cod from boats.

Boats: Boats are difficult to hire but there are one or two in Embo which is three miles from Dornoch.

Tackle: W.A. Macdonald, Castle Street, Dornoch.

Season for fishing: April-September.

Tain

Tain lies on the south side of the Dornoch Firth and gives access to excellent sea trout fishing, both shore and boat, in sheltered waters of the Firth.

Types of fish: Shore – wrasse, flatfish, pollack, mackerel. Boat – haddock, cod, skate, mackerel.

Boats: Available in Balintore, 6 miles from Tain.

Bait: Available from the shore.

Tackle: R. McLeod & Sons, 14 Lamington Street, Tain.

Further information from: G. McLeod, 14 Lamington Street, Tain.

Balintore

The village of Balintore, near Tain, has over the past 4 years increased in status and is now one of the recognised centres for big catches. Catches of up to 1,000lbs of cod and ling have been made (8 anglers) in a single morning's fishing.

Types of fish: Cod, ling, wrasse, pollack and mackerel.
Season from mid-April to beginning of November.

Portmahomack

This is a fishing village well situated in a small bay on the southern shore of the Dornoch Firth, 9 miles east of Tain and 17 miles from Invergordon to the south. There is a well-protected harbour and a good, safe sandy beach.

Types of fish: Cod from the shore. Haddock and cod from boats.

Tackle: Available at Tain.

Season for fishing: Spring to Autumn.

North Kessock, Avoch and Fortrose

These villages lie along the north-west side of the Moray Firth north of Inverness. This sheltered sea loch provides good fishing.

WESTERN ISLES

Area Tourist Board

Outer Hebrides Tourist Board,
Area Tourist Officer,
Outer Hebrides Tourist Board,
4 South Beach Street,
Stornoway,
Isle of Lewis PA87 2XY.
Tel: Stornoway (0851) 3088.

**RIVER PURIFICATION AUTHORITY
WESTERN ISLES ISLAND AREA**
(No formal Board constituted)

LOCHS

Water	Location	Species	Season	Permit available from	Other information
Breugach	Stornoway	Brown Trout	15 Mar. to 6 Oct.	The Sports Shop, 6 North Beach Street, Stornoway.	Two boats available.
Keose (and other lochs in Keose Glebe fishings	10 mls South of Stornoway	Brown Trout	15 Mar. to 30 Sept.	M. Morrison, 'Handa', 18 Keose Glebe, Lochs, Isle of Lewis PA86 9JX. Sports Shop, North Beach, Stornoway, Isle of Lewis.	Four boats, rods, tackle, life jackets, dinner, bed & breakfast at 'Handa', 18 Keose Glebe. No Sunday fishing.
BENBECULA Langavat (Heorovay - Olavat) and numerous other lochs	Benbecula	Sea Trout Salmon Brown Trout	1 Feb. to 31 Oct. 15 Mar.-30 Sept.	Bornish Stores, Tel: 08785-366. Campbell Sports Shop. Wool Shop, Creagorry. Orasay Inn, Carnan, Tel: 298.	Fly only. Boats available.
SOUTH UIST All hill and Machair Lochs	South Uist	Salmon Sea Trout Brown Trout	Jul.-Oct. Apr.-Sept.	Resident Manager, Lochboisdale Hotel, Lochboisdale, South Uist. Tel: Lochboisdale (08784) 367.	Fourteen boats available on lochs. Fly fishing only.

WESTERN ISLES

Sea Angling
The Western Isles

The Western Isles form a north-south chain of islands off the west coast of Scotland. Separated from the mainland by the Minches, much of their rod and line fishing remains to be discovered, not only due to a lack of boats in the area, but also due to a lack of communications between and within the islands. Car ferries run from Oban and Ullapool on the mainland and Uig on Skye. Regular air services to Barra, Stornoway, for Lewis and Harris and Benbecula for the Uists.

Isle of Harris (Tarbert)
The largest community on the southern part of the largest of the Hebridean islands, Tarbert stands on a very narrow neck of land where the Atlantic and the Minch are separated by only a few hundred yards of land. It is the terminal for the car ferry from Uig on Skye and Lochmaddy on North Uist.

Types of fish: Boat – mackerel, ling, coalfish, cod, rays, pollack and conger. Shore – plaice, haddock and flounder.
Boats: Check with Tourist Information Centre, Tarbert (0859) 2011.
Bait: Mussels available on the shore, lugworm, cockles.
Season for fishing: May- October.
Further information from: Tourist Centre, Tarbert.
Isle of Lewis (Stornoway)
Stornoway, the only town in the Outer Hebrides, is easily accessible by air from Glasgow Airport (1 hour) and Inverness (25 mins.); there is also a drive-on car ferry service from Ullapool (3½ hours crossing). Another car ferry service connects Uig (Skye) to Tarbert (Harris), which is only an hour's drive from Stornoway. Stornoway is now recognised as a mecca for sea angling in Scotland. There is an enthusiastic sea angling club with club boats and licensed premises which overlook the harbour. Each August the club runs the Western Isles (Open) Sea Angling

Championships. Many skate over the 'ton' have been caught, the heaviest so far being 192 lbs. The Scottish blueshark record of 85½ lbs. was off Stornoway in August 1972. Visiting anglers may become temporary members of the Stornoway Club (one minute from the town hall) and can make arrangements for fishing trips with club members in the club boats. Accommodation can be arranged through the Wester Isles Tourist Board, Administration and Information Centre, 4 South Beach Street, Tel: Stornoway (0851) 3088.

Types of fish: Conger, cod, skate, rays, ling, pollack, whiting, dabs, bluemouth, flounder, wrasse, haddock.

Tackle: Available from The Sports Shop, 6 North Beach Street, Stornoway, Isle of Lewis, Tel: 0851 5464 and C. Morrison & Sons, Point Street, Stornoway. C. Engebret & Co., Sandwick Road.

Bait: Mussels in harbour area; mackerel from local boats.

NORTHERN ISLES

Area Tourist Boards

Orkney Tourist Board,
Information Centre,
Broad Street, Kirkwall,
Orkney KW15 1DH.
Tel: Kirkwall (0856) 2856.

Shetland Tourist Organisation
Area Tourist Officer,
Shetland Tourist Organisation,
Information Centre,
Market Cross, Lerwick,
Sheltand ZE1 0LU.
Tel: Lerwick (0595) 3434.

**PURIFICATION AUTHORITY
ORKNEY ISLANDS AREA
SHETLAND ISLANDS AREA**
(No formal Boards constituted)

LOCHS

Water	Location	Species	Season	Permit available from	Other information
ORKNEY Boardhouse	Mainland	Brown Trout	15 Mar.-6 Oct.	None required	Boats available locally. All legal methods permitted. Anglers are recommended to join Orkney Trout Fishing Association, Kirkwall, who make facilities available to visitors.
Harray	Mainland	Brown Trout	15 Mar.-6 Oct.	Merkister Hotel, Tel: 085 677 366.	See Orkney for further information.
Hundland	Mainland	Brown Trout	15 Mar.-6 Oct.	None required	See Orkney for further information.
Kirbister	Mainland	Brown Trout	15 Mar.-6 Oct.	None required	See Orkney for further information.
Stenness	Mainland	Sea Trout Brown Trout	25 Feb.-31 Oct. 15 Mar.-6 Oct.	None required.	See Orkney for further information.
Swannay	Mainland	Brown Trout	15 Mar.-6 Oct.	None required	See Orkney for further information.
SHETLAND 1000 lochs & voes	Sheltand Islands	Sea Trout Brown Trout	25 Feb.-31 Oct. 15 Mar.-6 Oct.	Shetland Anglers Association, 3 Gladstone Terrace, Lerwick, Shetland.	

NORTHERN ISLES

Orkney

The waters around Orkney attract many sea anglers each year as big skate, halibut and ling are there for the taking. Ling of 36 lbs. skate of 214 lbs. taken by Jan Olsson of Sweden and the former British record halibut (161½lbs.) taken by ex-Provost Knight of Stromness provide the bait which attracts anglers to these waters. The Old Man of Hoy, Scapa Flow and Marwick Head are well-known names to sea anglers. The Brough of Birsay, Costa Head and the Eday and Stronsay Firths are equally well known as marks for big halibut and skate. Fishing from Kirkwall or Stromness, there is easy access to Scapa Flow where wrecks of the German Fleet of the First World War provide homes for large ling and conger. In the fish rich sea surrounding Orkney the angler will find some excellent shore fishing, nearly all of which remains to be discovered. Furthermore, skate of over 100 lbs. are still common while specimens of 200 lbs. have been recorded. More halibut have been caught in the waters to the south separating Orkney from the mainland than elsewhere in the U.K. Shark have also been sighted and hooked but none so far have been landed. Around the islands, in bays and firths, there is excellent sport for the specimen fish hunter and the Orcadians are eager to help sea anglers share the sport they enjoy. There is a regular car ferry service from Scrabster (Thurso) to Orkney and daily air services from Edinburgh, Glasgow and other points of the U.K.

Types of fish: Sea trout, plaice, pollack and coalfish, mackerel, wrasse from the shore. Skate, halibut, ling, cod, pollack, haddock, coalfish, plaice and dogfish from the boats.

Boats: Mr. Hay, Castlehill, Birsay, Tel. (085672) 270; Harray Loch - Merkister Hotel, Tel. (085 677) 366.
Tackle: available from Stromness and Kirkwall.

Bait: Available from most beaches and piers.

Season for fishing: June- October.

Further information from: Orkney Tourist Board Information Centre, Broad Street, Kirkwall KW15 1NX, Tel: (0856) 2856.

Shetland
The Shetlands offer the best skate fishing to be had in Europe;

during the years 1970-74 more than 250 skate over 100 lbs. were caught. These included a European record of 226½ lbs., and 12 other skate over 190 lbs. During the same period, Shetland held nine British records, ten Scottish records and six European records, giving some indication that the general fishing is of no mean standard. Halibut and porbeagle of over 300 lbs. have been taken commercially in the Sumburgh area with porbeagle shark now being landed by anglers from this area. The Scottish record porbeagle shark of 450 lbs. has been landed here and bigger fish have been taken by commercial boat. Shore- fishing remains for the most part to be discovered.

Types of fish: Shore – coalfish, pollack, dogfish, mackerel, dabs, conger and cod. Boat – skate, halibut, ling, cod, tusk, haddock,

whiting, coalfish, pollack, dogfish, porbeagle shark, Norway haddock, gurnard, mackerel, cuckoo and ballan wrasse.

Boats: Many boats available for hire throughout the islands. Boats can also be arranged through the Shetland Tourist Organisation, Information Centre, Lerwick, Shetland.

Tackle: Available from J.A. Manson, 88 Commercial Street, Lerwick and Cee & Jays, 5 Commercial Road, Lerwick. 30 - 50 lb. tackle can normally be hired with the boat through the Shetland Tourist Organisation.

Bait: Fresh, frozen or salted fish bait available from fishmongers. Worm bait, crabs, etc. from beaches.

Season for fishing: Limited to May to October by weather conditions.

Mackerel make an ideal bait for many predatory sea fish.

Please mention this Pastime Publications Guide

Wick, Caithness

MAPS

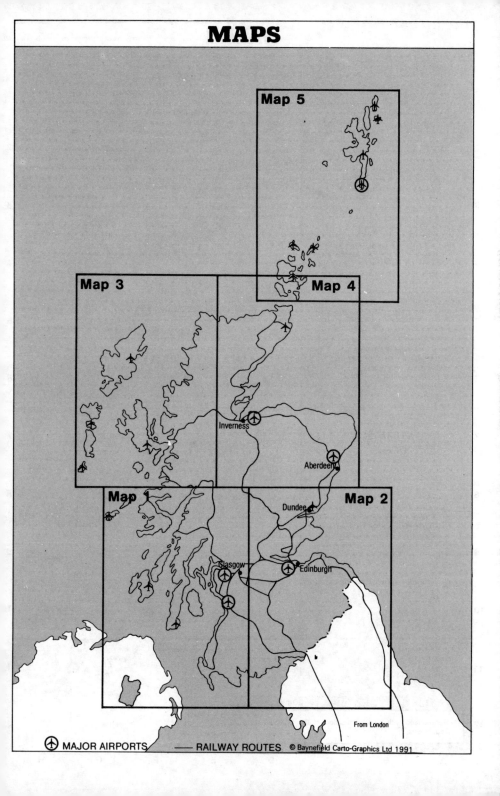

Map 5

Map 3

Map 4

Inverness

Aberdeen

Map 1

Map 2

Dundee

Glasgow

Edinburgh

From London

⊕ MAJOR AIRPORTS —— RAILWAY ROUTES © Baynefield Carto-Graphics Ltd 1991

MAP 1

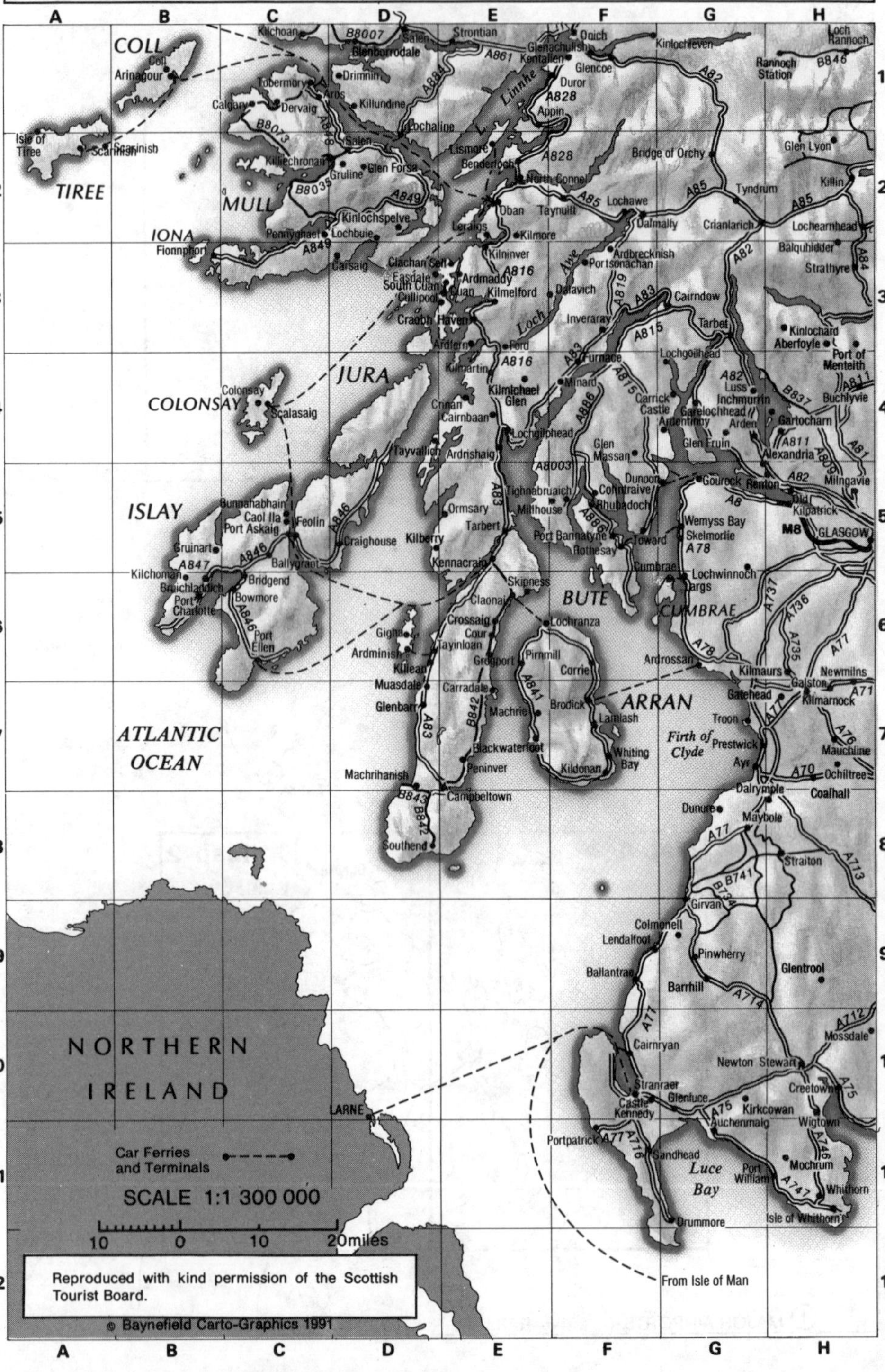
COLL
Coll
Arinagour
TIREE
Isle of Tiree
Scarinish
MULL
IONA
Fionnphort
Tobermory
Dervaig
Calgary
Aros
Killundine
Drimnin
Salen
Killiechronan
Gruline
Glen Forsa
Kinlochspelve
Pennyghael
Lochbuie
Carsaig
Lochaline
Kilchoan
Glenborrodale
Strontian
Glenachulish
Kentallen
Onich
Glencoe
Kinlochleven
Duror
Appin
Lismore
Benderloch
North Connel
Oban
Taynuilt
Lochawe
Dalmally
Kilmore
Kilninver
Clachan Seil
Easdale
South Cuan
Cuan
Cullipool
Ardmaddy
Kilmelford
Craobh Haven
Ardfern
Ford
Kilmartin
Kilmichael Glen
Crinan
Cairnbaan
Lochgilphead
Ardrishaig
Tayvallich
Loch Linnhe
Loch Awe
Dalavich
Portsonachan
Ardbrecknish
Inveraray
Furnace
Minard
Cairndow
Tarbet
Lochgoilhead
Carrick Castle
Ardentinny
Garelochhead
Luss
Inchmurrin
Arden
Glen Fruin
Alexandria
Gartocharn
Glen Massan
Colintraive
Rhubadoch
Tighnabruaich
Millhouse
Dunoon
Gourock
Renton
Milngavie
Old Kilpatrick
GLASGOW
Toward
Port Bannatyne
Rothesay
BUTE
Wemyss Bay
Skelmorlie
Cumbrae
Largs
CUMBRAE
Lochwinnoch
JURA
COLONSAY
Colonsay
Scalasaig
ISLAY
Bunnahabhain
Caol Ila
Port Askaig
Feolin
Craighouse
Gruinart
Kilchoman
Ballygrant
Bridgend
Bruichladdich
Port Charlotte
Bowmore
Port Ellen
Gigha
Ardminish
Kilberry
Ormsary
Tarbert
Kennacraig
Skipness
Claonaig
Crossaig
Cour
Tayinloan
Killean
Muasdale
Glenbarr
Grogport
Carradale
Machrihanish
Campbeltown
Southend
Peninver
Lochranza
Pirnmill
Corrie
Brodick
ARRAN
Lamlash
Machrie
Blackwaterfoot
Whiting Bay
Kildonan
Ardrossan
Kilmaurs
Galston
Newmilns
Gatehead
Kilmarnock
Troon
Prestwick
Ayr
Mauchline
Ochiltree
Firth of Clyde
Dalrymple
Coalhall
Dunure
Maybole
Straiton
Girvan
Colmonell
Lendalfoot
Pinwherry
Glentrool
Ballantrae
Barrhill
Cairnryan
Mossdale
Newton Stewart
Stranraer
Glenluce
Creetown
Castle Kennedy
Kirkcowan
Auchenmalg
Wigtown
Portpatrick
Sandhead
Luce Bay
Port William
Mochrum
Whithorn
Drummore
Isle of Whithorn
From Isle of Man
Bridge of Orchy
Rannoch Station
Loch Rannoch
Glen Lyon
Tyndrum
Killin
Crianlarich
Lochearnhead
Balquhidder
Strathyre
Kinlochard
Aberfoyle
Port of Menteith
Buchlyvie
ATLANTIC OCEAN
NORTHERN IRELAND
LARNE
Car Ferries and Terminals
SCALE 1:1 300 000
10 0 10 20miles
A B C D E F G H
1 2 3 4 5 6 7 8 9 10 11 12
Reproduced with kind permission of the Scottish Tourist Board.
© Baynefield Carto-Graphics 1991

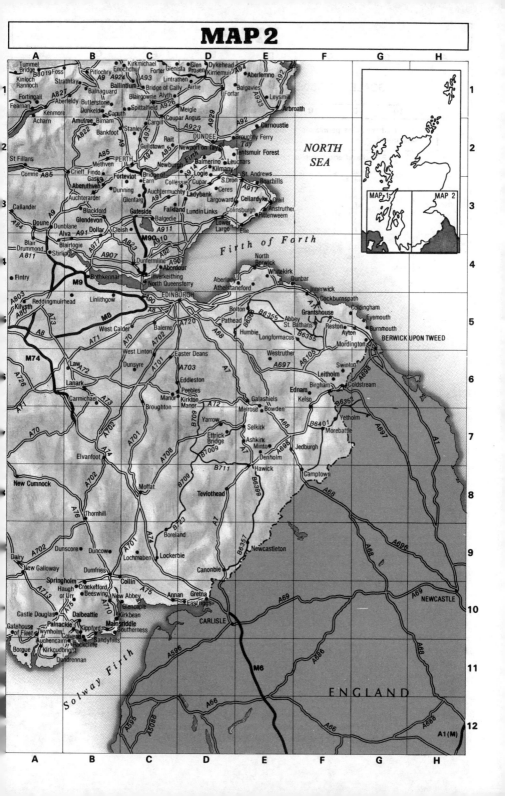

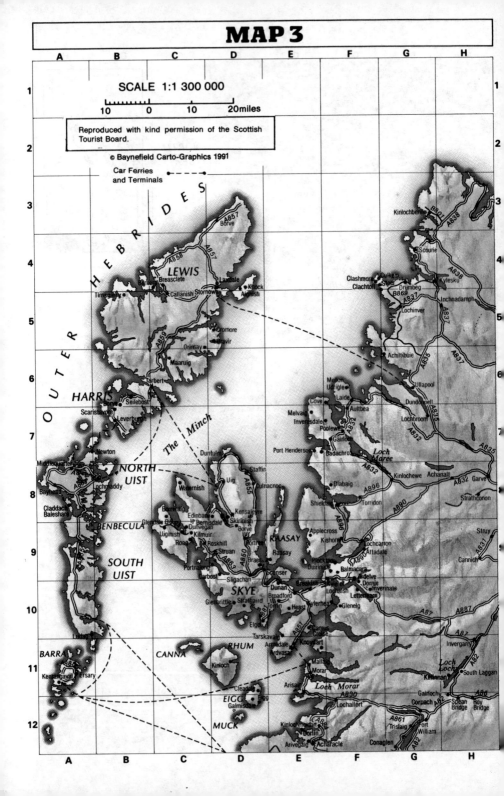

MAP 4

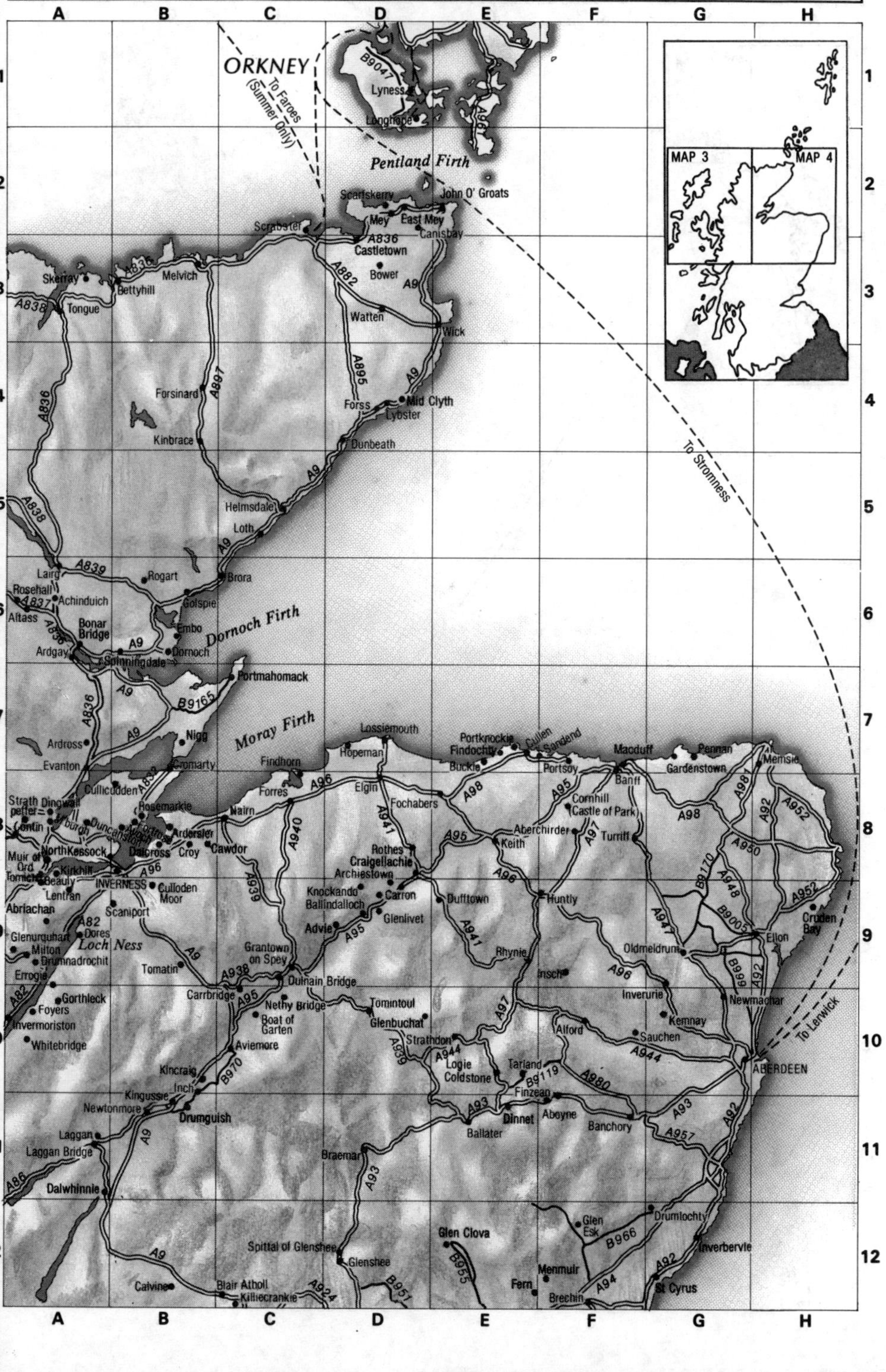
A
B
C
D
E
F
G
H
1
2
3
4
5
6
7
8
9
10
11
12
ORKNEY
To Faroes (Summer Only)
B9047
Lyness
Longhope
A961
Pentland Firth
Scarfskerry
John O' Groats
Mey
East Mey
Scrabster
A836
Canisbay
Castletown
Skerray
A836
Melvich
Bettyhill
A838
Tongue
A882
Bower
A9
Watten
Wick
A897
A895
A836
Forsinard
A9
Mid Clyth
Forss
Lybster
Kinbrace
Dunbeath
A9
To Stromness
A838
Helmsdale
Loth
A9
Lairg
A839
Rogart
Brora
Rosehall
A837
Achinduich
Golspie
Altass
A836
Bonar Bridge
Embo
Dornoch Firth
A9
Ardgay
Dornoch
Spinningdale
Portmahomack
A9
A836
B9165
A9
Moray Firth
Ardross
Nigg
Lossiemouth
Portknockie
Cullen
Sandend
Hopeman
Findochty
Macduff
Pennan
Evanton
Cromarty
A832
Findhorn
Buckie
Portsoy
Gardenstown
Memsie
Culicudden
Forres
A96
Elgin
A98
Banff
Strath peffer
Dingwall
Rosemarkie
Nairn
A940
Fochabers
A95
Cornhill (Castle of Park)
A98
A981
A92
A952
Contin
Duncanston
Fortrose
Ardersier
A941
Aberchirder
A97
Turriff
Muir of Ord
North Kessock
Dalcross
Croy
Cawdor
Rothes
Craigellachie
Archiestown
A95
Keith
A950
Tomich
Kirkhill
Beauly
A96
A939
A96
B9170
A948
Lentran
INVERNESS
Culloden Moor
Knockando
Ballindalloch
Carron
Dufftown
Huntly
A952
Abriachan
Scaniport
Glenlivet
A941
A947
B9005
Cruden Bay
Glenurquhart
A82
Dores
Advie
A95
Ellon
Milton
Drumnadrochit
Loch Ness
A9
Grantown on Spey
Rhynie
Oldmeldrum
Errogie
Tomatin
A938
Dulnain Bridge
Insch
A96
B999
A92
A82
Gorthleck
Carrbridge
A95
Nethy Bridge
Tomintoul
A97
Inverurie
Newmachar
Foyers
Boat of Garten
Glenbuchat
Kemnay
Invermoriston
Aviemore
A939
Strathdon
Alford
Sauchen
To Lerwick
Whitebridge
A944
A944
Kincraig
B970
Logie Coldstone
Tarland
B9119
A980
ABERDEEN
Inch
Kingussie
Finzean
Newtonmore
Drumguish
A93
Dinnet
Aboyne
Banchory
A93
A9
Ballater
A957
Laggan
Laggan Bridge
Braemar
A92
A86
A93
Dalwhinnie
Drumlochty
Glen Esk
B966
Glen Clova
Spittal of Glenshee
B955
Inverbervie
A9
Glenshee
Menmuir
A92
Calvine
Blair Atholl
A924
B951
Fern
A94
St Cyrus
Killiecrankie
Brechin
MAP 3
MAP 4

MAP 5

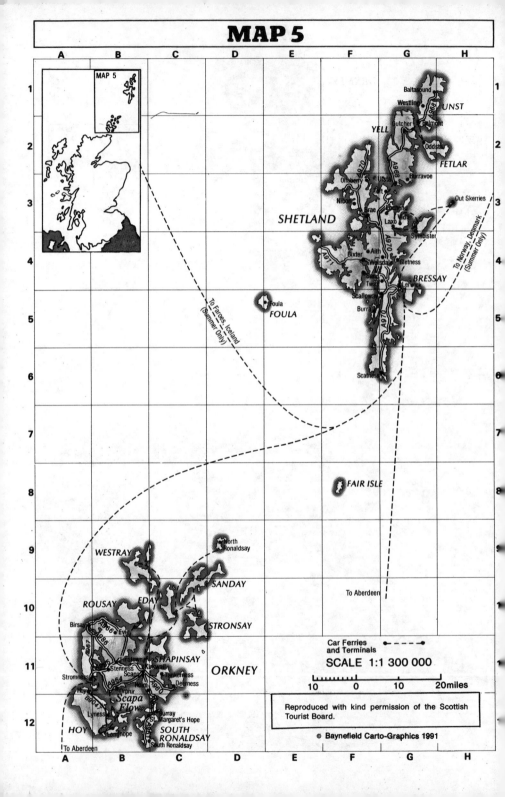